The
SAMHAIN
SPELL for
BOOK
BUSY NEW
WITCHES

LILY
NIGHTSHADE

Table of Contents

Table of Contents

CHAPTER 3: BLACK CAT LUCK . .44

CHAPTER 4: LANTERN PATHS & TRAVEL WARDS. .58

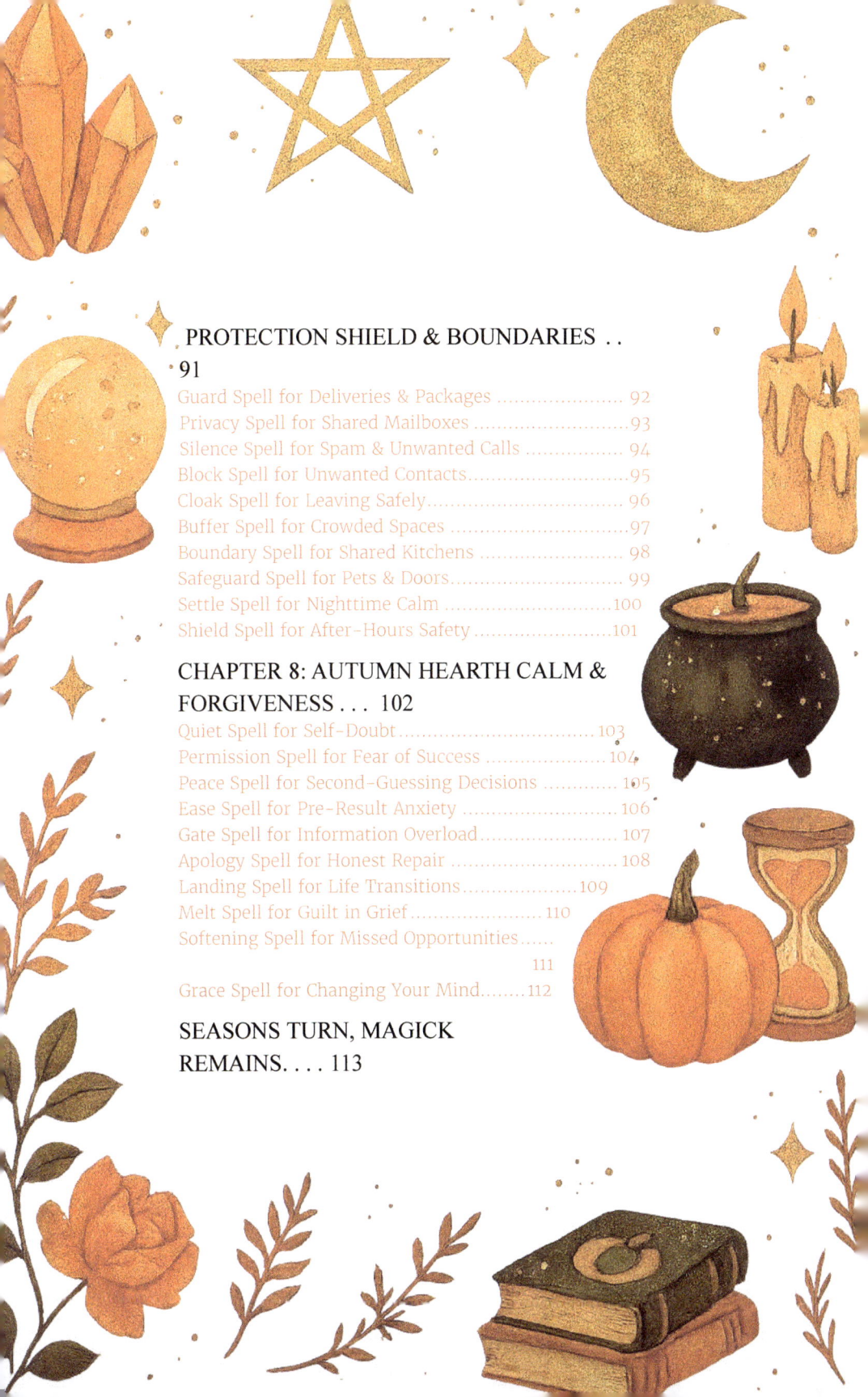

PROTECTION SHIELD & BOUNDARIES .. 91

CHAPTER 8: AUTUMN HEARTH CALM & FORGIVENESS . . . 102

SEASONS TURN, MAGICK REMAINS. . . . 113

Disclaimer and Legal Notice

Introduction

Maybe you are holding this book because something has been tugging at you. A quiet whisper that says there is more to life than endless scrolling, more than anxious waiting for texts, more than walking into rooms and feeling like you do not belong. Maybe you are curious about witchcraft but every time you searched online you found rules, gatekeeping, and complicated rituals that left you overwhelmed. Maybe you have wondered if magick is only for people with years of study, rare herbs, or expensive tools.

With this book, **you do not need to join a coven or call on deities**. or follow Wicca or believe in reincarnation, past lives, or anything outside your comfort zone.

I know those feelings because I have lived them. I still remember my first date after a long spell of swiping. My stomach was in knots, my head was loud with doubt, and I desperately wanted my intuition to speak clearly. I mixed vinegar, salt, and a single bay leaf into a quick ritual. For the first time I walked into that coffee shop with my senses sharp and my confidence steady. That was the beginning of discovering that magick could be simple, practical, and powerful.

That is what this book gives you. Not long ceremonies. Only three-minute spells that meet you in your real life.

When texts go silent and your mind spins in circles, you will find a spell to soothe your worry to help you respond with calm.

When you are meeting someone new and want your edges clear, you will learn a boundary spell with salt, pepper, and a bay leaf that keeps your heart open while still protected.

Each of these spells is fast, safe, and designed for the life you are already living. You can do them in a kitchen, a dorm room, or a small apartment. You can swap candles for electronic lights if fire is not allowed. You can substitute herbs with what you have on hand. Witchcraft is not about perfection. It is about intention, focus, & action.

Samhain is the perfect time to begin. It is the witch's new year, when the veil is thin and transformation is strongest. But these spells are not only for one season. They are written to walk beside you all year long, through spring's growth, summer's energy, autumn's harvest, and winter's stillness.

And if this book was gifted to you, know this: you are deeply valued. Someone saw your potential and wanted to place real tools of empowerment in your hands.

This is not just a spellbook. It is a companion, a guide, and a reminder that you are the magick. The spark is already within you. These pages simply help you light it.

Take a breath. Turn the page. Your journey has already begun.

Opening the Door

Welcome, traveler of twilight.

My name is Lily, and I have walked the winding path of witchcraft for many years. My beginning was not dramatic or sudden. It came gently, like the hush of wind through autumn trees, carrying both grief and wonder in its arms. I did not find magic in dusty libraries or fantasy films, but in silence, in longing, and in the way nature seemed to whisper back when I spoke.

When the Veil First Stirred

I was sixteen when my grandmother died. She was the center of our family, the kind of woman whose laughter filled even the quietest corners. After she passed, the world felt gray. One evening, I wandered into her garden, where rosemary, roses, and damp soil still carried her presence.

I sat by the rosemary bush and wept, telling her all the words I could no longer say. Suddenly, a breeze rose and wrapped me in that sharp, green scent. It felt as if the plant itself had leaned down to listen. For the first time in weeks, I did not feel alone. I understand now that this was magic — not a spell with candles or charms, but an open door between worlds, a moment of communion with what lingers beyond sight.

What Drew Me to the Craft

After that night, I started noticing patterns. Flames seemed to dance in answer to my questions, storms mirrored my moods, and dreams deepened when I placed stones beneath my pillow. Magic was not about control, but about attunement — listening, aligning, and weaving myself into the living rhythm of the world.

At first, it was medicine for my grief. Later, it became a way of reclaiming joy, courage, and meaning. Spells were not just rituals; they were acts of connection, reminders that possibility is always near if you are willing to reach for it.

Why This Book Exists

Over the years, I have met countless people who feel drawn to witchcraft but hesitate at the threshold. They worry it is too complicated, or that they need rare tools and years of study. Some fear they are not "real witches." I wrote this book for them, and for you.

This Samhain Spell Book is kin to my 3 Minute Spell Book. Both carry the same heart: magic should be simple, personal, and woven into daily life. But here, we focus on Samhain — the season of endings and beginnings, when the veil thins and the ancestors draw near. These pages hold short, powerful rituals that honor release, remembrance, and renewal.

You do not need exotic ingredients. You only need presence, intention, and the courage to step into your own power.

What Awaits You Here

Inside you will find spells that fit easily into your days, rituals that take only moments but shift energy in lasting ways. These practices honor the spirit of Samhain: protection, gratitude, letting go of the old, and inviting the new.

If you are reading this now, the path has already opened for you. Whether you came here curious, grieving, or simply hungry for meaning, trust that this book found you at the right time. Samhain is a doorway, and you are ready to step through.

Light a candle. Take a breath. Together, we will walk into the liminal space where endings whisper to beginnings, and where magic waits patiently for you.

The Living Current of Magic

Magic does not live in tools alone. Herbs, crystals, and candles are beautiful allies, but they are not the source. Magic breathes in the rustle of bare branches, in the crackle of bonfires, in the rhythm of waves, and in the quickening of your own heartbeat when you whisper a wish.

To cast a spell is not to bend the universe but to move with it. It is the act of focusing your energy, aligning with intention, and sending it out like ripples across still water. Tools are only amplifiers. The true current of power has always been within you.

The Ground Beneath Us

To walk the witch's path is to honor both roots and branches: the ancestors who came before, the world we live in now, and the future we are shaping with every choice. A foundation grounded in history, respect, and awareness gives depth to every charm you weave.

That is why, before we turn to spells and rituals, we will pause here to explore the essence of the craft. Together we will clear away myths, untangle the threads between witchcraft and Wicca, and reflect on the ethics that keep our practice strong. These are not restrictions. They are stepping stones, giving you firm ground to stand on as you begin to create, release, and transform.

> When you understand this foundation, every spell becomes more than a ritual. It becomes a conversation with the world, and a promise to yourself.

What Spellcasting Truly Is

Spellcasting is not a secret locked away in ancient grimoires. It is focused intention — the art of taking a thought or desire and shaping it into reality. In fact, everyone casts spells without calling them spells. When you whisper a wish before blowing out candles, you are casting. When you slip a lucky charm into your pocket before a test, you are casting. When you visualize your success and feel your whole body align with that vision, you are casting.

The world may not see these acts, but inside they are powerful. They are energy put to work. And at Samhain, when the veil thins, the intentions we send out move even more swiftly, carried by the season's tide of endings and beginnings.

The Nature of Energy

Magic is the current flowing through every living and unliving thing. It is not good or bad. It is as neutral as fire: it can warm your home or reduce it to ash. The morality of magic comes from the one directing it.

You have felt energy already. The shiver when someone steps too close before touching you, the heaviness in a room after an argument, the calmness of a forest path in autumn. That is energy brushing against yours. Spells simply gather, shape, and release that current with clarity.

We are not the only ones who do this. Yogis guide breath to move energy, Reiki practitioners channel it through the palms, monks raise it with chants, and tai chi practitioners shape it through slow, deliberate movement. These are cousins to spellwork. They remind us that energy is not abstract, not fantasy — it is something we feel, direct, and use every day.

Roots of Spellcasting

The word spell comes from the Anglo-Saxon spel, meaning story or saying. From the beginning, spells were words woven with power. Ancient Egyptians carved them into tomb walls to guide souls. Norse folk etched runes into wood and stone as protections. Healers whispered charms over herbs and fire.

But history also shows the shadows: persecution, fear, and trials. Books like the Malleus Maleficarum branded witches dangerous, and Salem in 1692 saw lives destroyed by fear. Yet magic survived. It hid in kitchens, in gardens, in whispered blessings before meals or over sick children.

At Samhain, I often think of those who kept the craft alive. Ancestors who carried the flame quietly so that we could practice openly now. Spellcasting is as old as storytelling, as natural as breathing, and each time we cast, we add our voice to that unbroken thread.

Hedge Witches and Plant Allies

Among the many paths of witchcraft, hedge witches are the threshold walkers, those who step between this world and the Otherworld. Their craft is liminal: rooted in dreams, spirits, and the wisdom of plants. They work with herbs, salves, teas, and charms, treating plants as partners.

Some hedge witches enter altered states to cross the veil. Historically, mushrooms, nightshades, and ointments carried them into visions. These were never toys but sacred allies, dangerous if misused, powerful when respected. Today, many hedge witches prefer trance drumming, chanting, or lucid dreaming.

On Samhain, when the veil is already thin, hedge witches remind us that the boundary between seen and unseen is always porous. Their craft teaches us that magic is not just ritual — it is relationship: with plants, with spirits, and with the mysteries that walk beside us.

Many Paths Through the Forest

There is no single way to be a witch. The craft is a forest of many trails:

◊ Elemental Witches draw on earth, air, fire, and water. Green witches turn to herbs and crystals, sea witches to tides and storms, hearth witches to kitchen fire and home.

◊ Secular Witches work without deities, grounding their craft in symbols, metaphors, and intention.

◊ Hedge Witches cross thresholds, working with plants, spirits, and dreams. Some journey with plant allies, others with meditation.

◊ Eclectic Witches gather from many places, weaving a practice that is fluid and personal.

◊ Traditional Witches walk older, structured paths, sometimes passed down through family or folk lineage.

No path is more authentic than another. At Samhain, when the forest grows quiet and the dead draw near, you may feel called to one of these trails. Or you may wander between them. The only true path is the one that nourishes your spirit.

Claiming Your Power

Spells are not shortcuts. They do not erase free will or bend the universe like clay. They are invitations. They are the way we align ourselves with possibility and send our energy into the world with purpose.

The spark of magic already burns within you. This book is here to help you tend that fire, shape it, and let it grow. Remember: you are not chasing magic outside yourself. You are remembering what is already yours.

Preparing a Spell: Crafting and Casting

Every spell has two halves: crafting and casting. Crafting is preparing the ground. Casting is planting the seed.

When I craft, I begin by clearing space. Sometimes it is as simple as brushing leaves from a stone outdoors. Sometimes it is wiping down my altar inside. I cleanse by clapping, lighting incense, or imagining light sweeping through the area like a broom.

Then I create a circle of protection. Not walls, but intention. Some call on gods or spirits. I imagine a soft ring of fire, golden and steady, humming around me. Inside it, I feel safe, grounded, and ready.

Casting is when intention takes form. Lighting a candle, tying a cord, whispering a spell. When I am finished, I always close the circle, thanking the energy and letting it return to the earth.

Where Magic Happens

Spells do not need temples or grand altars. They can happen anywhere you feel safe and focused. I have stirred spells into soup in my kitchen, whispered them in baths with rose petals, and sent them into the night air under the full moon.

One of my first spells was secret. A shoebox lid as altar, a kitchen candle, and wildflowers pressed in a schoolbook. It was uneven, but it worked because it carried intention.

At Samhain, I often cast outdoors, near bonfires or in candlelit rooms with photos of ancestors. These places feel alive with presence, and intention flows more easily. But the truth is: the best place is wherever you are fully present.

Building an Altar

An altar is your stage, your workbench, your doorway. It can be as grand as a permanent table or as simple as a stone on the ground. Some witches place salt for earth, incense for air, a candle for fire, and a cup of water. Others add feathers, shells, crystals, or photos of ancestors.

One Samhain night, I built an altar of driftwood, apples, and candles. When the wind lifted the flames and the tide lapped close, I felt as if the sea itself had joined in. That is the point of an altar: presence, not perfection. Let yours shift with the seasons, the moon, or your own moods.

Learning to Use Your Power

Before casting, you must learn to center, raise, and ground.

◊ Centering is balance. Breathe deeply, imagine a glowing sphere of light in your core, and let it pulse with each breath.

◊ Raising is fuel. Chant, drum, dance, or focus. Borrow strength from crystals, the moon, or the season itself. At Samhain, I often raise energy by walking around a fire, letting its heat mingle with mine.

◊ Grounding is release. After casting, press your palms to soil, or imagine roots from your feet sinking deep into the earth. On each exhale, let the extra energy flow away, leaving you steady again.

This rhythm will keep your magic powerful without draining you.

Solitary or Shared Spellwork

Do you need a coven? No. Solitary practice is powerful and personal. But some witches find joy in circles.

Covens are structured, often with leaders and rituals. They can be warm or rigid. Circles are looser, gatherings under the moon or around a fire to share magic and community. At Samhain, many witches gather to honor ancestors together, while others light a single candle alone. Both are valid.

The only rule is this: never remain where you feel unsafe or unwelcome. Magic thrives where you feel free.

Casting is not complicated. It is a dance between your energy and the world. At Samhain, that dance feels closer, sharper, more alive. Start small. Whisper your wish into an apple before eating it. Light a candle for your ancestors. Stir soup with intention.

Over time, your craft will deepen, your energy will flow more easily, and you will find your rhythm.

Because in the end, every spell begins not with tools or circles, but with you.

Calendars, Seasons, and Sacred Tools

When I first began, I lit candles whenever the mood struck and whispered wishes into the air between errands. Sometimes the magic moved, sometimes it stalled. I did not understand that I was pushing against the river. Magic, like breath, follows rhythm. The earth turns through seasons, the moon swells and thins, the sun marks solstices and equinoxes. When I began to cast in step with those cycles, my spells felt carried, as if the world itself had taken my hand.

The Wheel of the Year

The Wheel of the Year turns through eight festivals called sabbats. Each is a doorway into a specific flavor of energy. Step through and you feel the season shaping your spell for you.

Samhain

October 31 in the northern hemisphere. The witch's New Year, last harvest, the veil is thin and the ancestors draw near. I light a single candle beside a bowl of apples and set out photos of those I love. The quiet feels alive, like a room holding its breath. Begin here: Place a photo or keepsake on a small ancestor altar. Light a candle. Speak their names and thank them. That is a spell.

Yule

Winter solstice, the longest night. A promise that light returns. One hard winter I kept vigil with one candle until dawn. When the first light touched the windowsill, I felt hope settle into my bones. Begin here: Write what you release on small paper, burn it safely, then write one hope for the year and keep it on your altar until spring.

Imbolc

February 1, the first quickening beneath the frost. Clearing, creativity, new fire. I open the windows, sweep corners, and light a white candle. The room exhales and so do I. Begin here: Clean one corner. Light a white candle. Speak a single creative goal aloud as if planting a seed.

Ostara

Spring equinox, day and night in balance. Renewal and steady growth. I press seeds into soil with a whispered intention for each. By midsummer, basil becomes dinner seasoned with a spell. Begin here: Plant something small in a pot. Name what you want to grow as you cover the seed.

Beltane

May 1, fire, love, bright beginnings. I tie ribbons to a branch, each one a wish for joy, courage, or connection. Wind lifts them like prayer flags. Begin here: Light a candle and move your body. Name one desire out loud. Celebrate your fire.

Litha

Summer solstice, the longest day. Vitality, gratitude, empowerment. I lie in the grass and let sunlight soak in. At night I write a gratitude list and feed it to a small flame. Begin here: Spend time in sunlight. Say one thing you are proud of this year.

Lughnasadh

August 1, first harvest, also called Lammas. Gratitude and preparation. I bake simple bread and knead thankfulness into the dough. Sharing it multiplies the blessing. Begin here: Share food with someone. Speak gratitude before you eat.

Mabon

Autumn equinox, balance returns. Second harvest and thanksgiving. I cook apples and squash and invite a friend to name three blessings. The room glows warmer than the oven. Begin here: Cook a seasonal meal. Before the first bite, say what you are grateful for.

The sun keeps the year. The moon teaches the month. Her phases are a simple road map for timing spells.

New Moon Blank page energy. Begin, seed, set intentions. Write a goal and place it beneath a candle.

Waxing Moon Growing energy. Choose spells for courage, momentum, creativity, luck. Charge a small charm each night on your windowsill.

Full Moon Peak energy. Charge crystals and tools, divine, make bolder moves. Stand in moonlight and speak your desire clearly.

Waning Moon Releasing energy. Cleanse, cut cords, end habits, clear clutter. Write what you release and burn it safely, scatter cool ashes in soil.

Dark Moon Quiet energy. Rest, reflect, protect. Journal in low light or sit in silence and listen.

The first time I made moon water, I set a glass outside under a round white moon. Drinking it at dawn felt like swallowing a star. Simple does not mean small.

Sacred Tools, Seasonal Rhythm

Tools do not create power. They focus the power that is already inside you and in the season around you.

Candle and Match Fire focuses attention and marks a beginning. At Samhain, a single flame beside an ancestor photo is more than enough.

Bowl and Salt Earth and vessel. A pinch of salt in a small bowl cleanses a space quickly. I keep mine near the door in autumn.

Cup and Water Offerings and blessing. Moon water in a cup becomes a quiet anointing before a ritual or a few drops on the threshold for protection.

String and Ribbon Knot magic. I tie three knots for protection on dark October nights and hang the ribbon on my altar until dawn.

Apple and Knife Samhain symbol and simple scrying. Cut safely across the middle to reveal the star and ask a question. Eat slowly and listen.

Choose one tool per spell and let the season provide the rest. Fallen leaves can become petitions. A backyard stone can be an altar. The cold night air can be your incense.

Why This Matters

These calendars and cycles are not rules. They are rhythms. When you cast inside them, you borrow the strength of tide and season. Your magic feels less like pushing and more like floating with a strong current. If you are beginning, choose one sabbat to honor, one moon cycle to follow, and one tool to dedicate. Small and sincere will always be enough.

Tools of the Craft

Tools do not hold power by themselves. They simply help focus and amplify the magic that is already within you. Many of these items have been used for centuries in sacred ways, but none are required to begin. Start with what you have, add slowly, and remember that intention is always the truest tool.

Book of Shadows

Your magical diary, a place to record spells, dreams, and reflections. Witches once kept hidden grimoires for safety. A blank notebook or a folder on your computer works just as well.

Altar Bowl

A vessel for offerings, herbs, salt, or water. Cultures from Greece to Egypt used bowls to hold sacred substances. Any dish you already own can become an altar bowl.

Mortar and Pestle

Used for grinding herbs and resins while infusing them with your energy. Apothecaries relied on this tool for centuries. A kitchen set or even your hands are enough to begin.

Candles

Flames symbolize focus and transformation. Fire rituals reach back to the earliest human gatherings. A single white candle or tea light can stand in for any color.

Crystals

Crystals store and radiate energy like batteries. Ancient healers worked with stones for balance and strength. Start with clear quartz and cleanse it often with water or moonlight.

Incense

Smoke purifies and shifts energy. Temples and sacred spaces across the world have burned incense for centuries. One stick or a small herb bundle is all you need.

Divination Tools

Tarot, runes, and pendulums help reveal patterns and strengthen intuition. Oracles and scrying practices have always guided seekers. Start by pulling a single card or asking a pendulum yes or no questions.

Besom (Broom)

Used to sweep away stagnant energy and mark sacred space.

Folklore placed besoms by doors for protection. A small broom dedicated to ritual will serve you well.

Poppets

Dolls made of cloth, wax, or clay to represent people or intentions. Folk traditions used them for healing and protection. Beginners can sew a simple doll and fill it with herbs.

Wand or Athame

Both channel energy, one outward, one symbolically. A fallen branch or even your finger can be your first wand. My first wand was a willow branch and I still keep it today.

Chalice

A cup that represents water, emotion, and creation. Ritual chalices appear across many cultures. Any cup you set aside for practice can serve this role.

Pentacle

A disc marked with a five-pointed star within a circle. It represents the four elements and spirit in balance. Beginners can draw one on paper to use for charging or protection.

Feathers

Symbols of air, spirit, and communication. Feathers were sacred in many traditions and often seen as divine messages. A feather you find can be cleansed and placed on your altar.

Anointing Oils

Oils infused with herbs and intention for blessing and protection. Ancient cultures used sacred oils for healing and ritual. Mix olive oil with kitchen herbs to make your own simple version.

Clothing and Adornment

What you wear shapes your energy. Some witches wear robes, others practice skyclad. Choose one item to wear only during ritual, even if it is just a scarf or pendant. Over time it will carry your energy and signal your body that it is time for magic.

Beginning Simply

You do not need every tool. Start with one. Watch a moon cycle, honor a single sabbat, dedicate one item of clothing. Each step connects you to the rhythm of the world. When you move with those rhythms, your spells flow more naturally, your practice feels stronger, and your heart feels more rooted. That is where your true power begins.

The Language of Spells

When I first began casting, I stumbled over the basics. Books spoke of cleansing, anointing, and charging as if I should already know. I didn't, and maybe you don't either. These are the foundations, the little rituals that make every spell stronger. Once you know them, you can read almost any spell and step right in.

Clear the Air

Every spell begins with cleansing. Witches have cleared spaces for centuries with smoke, salt, and sound because energy lingers like cobwebs. I clap my hands in the corners or burn a stick of incense, then say, "This space is clear, this space is mine." The moment the air feels lighter, the magic has already begun.

Wipe the Slate Clean

Tools carry traces of every hand that touched them. A crystal from a market, a candle from the store shelf, even a spoon from your kitchen deserves a reset. Pass it through smoke, rinse in saltwater, or imagine light pouring through it. You will feel the shift when it is ready.

Moon-Soaked Water

Water remembers. Many cultures saw it as sacred because it holds energy like a mirror. The first time I left a jar out under a full moon, it looked brighter the next morning, as if it had swallowed light. Place a bowl of water outside on the full moon and use it to bless, sip, or anoint. Even if clouds cover the sky, the moon will still find its way in.

Stone Recharge

Crystals are like batteries. When they are full, they hum. When they are tired, they dull. Leave them under the full moon, place them on soil, or hold one in your palm while breathing deeply until it feels alive again. That small vibration in your hand is its spark returning.

Breathing Life Back In

Magic fades with time. A jar or pendant will lose charge the way perfume loses scent. When that happens, repeat part of the spell: smoke it, anoint it, or speak the words again. The item will drink it up like water, and its power will return.

Oils of Power

To anoint is to bless. Priests, queens, and healers once used oils to make the ordinary sacred. For you, it can be as simple as dipping a finger in olive oil and tracing a symbol on a candle or on your skin. A single drop is enough to seal intention.

Through the Looking Glass

Scrying is the art of gazing into something until your mind quiets and images stir. Our ancestors used water, fire, and smoke. I often stare into a candle flame until shapes drift forward. You may see colors or nothing at first. The key is to trust that your intuition is speaking, even softly.

Wand in Hand

A wand is not about sparks or spectacle. It is focus. I think of mine as an extra finger pointing energy where it needs to go. When I trace a circle, I imagine a wall of light. When I point at a crystal, I picture energy flowing into it. A branch from the park can work as well as a carved wand if you treat it with care.

Breath Into Stone

Imbuing is the act of filling an object with your energy. The first time I tried, I held a pebble, whispered a wish, and felt it grow warm. That warmth was my intention sinking in. To do this, hold your item, breathe slowly, and imagine your desire glowing inside it.

Why These Steps Matter

These actions are not extras, they are the bones of spellwork. Cleansing clears space, purification wipes history, charging fills with energy, and imbuing seals intention. Oils bless, wands focus, scrying opens intuition, and recharging keeps tools alive. Practice these until they are second nature, like making tea. That is when magic begins to flow without effort

Chapter 1: Samhain Gateways

Ancestors, Shadow and Wishes

On Samhain, the old stories say the veil thins like breath on glass. Hearths were swept, candles lit, and plates set for those who came before. In some villages, doors were left slightly open to welcome kind spirits, while turnips and later pumpkins were carved to keep wanderers at bay. The night was not only scary, it was sacred. It was a crossroads where memory, courage, and new beginnings met.

Samhain is a doorway night. Doorways ask two questions. What do you keep out, and what do you invite in. These spells live right at that threshold. They help you draw boundaries with restless energy, listen privately to your heart, lay down old weight, soften family tension, release guilt, reset your path, name your aim, trust your instincts, warm your home, and stand steady in your own light.

Ancestor Boundary Spell for Unwanted Contact

I made this on a night when dreams felt crowded, like too many voices at one small table. I was grateful for my roots, but I needed sleep and space. I set a tiny circle of salt, lit a candle, and asked for respectful distance.

By the time the flame steadied, my room felt quiet and clear. It was not a rejection. It was a line. Love can have a fence and still be love.

WHEN TO PERFORM:

Samhain night or any Saturday after sunset

TIME TO ALLOT:

3 minutes

WHERE TO PERFORM:

Kitchen table or windowsill

INGREDIENTS/TOOLS:

- ◇ Tea light candle
- ◇ Small bowl of water
- ◇ White vinegar
- ◇ Sea salt
- ◇ Bay leaf

🌙 Optional: A sprig of rosemary. Not required, but adds an extra layer of protective clarity.

Directions

1. Place the candle on a safe surface. Never leave it unattended.
2. Add a splash of vinegar to the water and set the bowl beside the candle.
3. Sprinkle a small ring of salt around both, leaving a little gap facing your door.
4. Hold the bay leaf to your heart and say, "I honor you. I keep my peace."
5. Light the candle and speak softly, "Only kindness may cross this line."
6. Snuff the candle. Pour the bowl outside or down the drain to seal the boundary.

Stealth Remembrance Spell for Private Reflection

Grief and memory can be loud in a house full of people. I needed a way to remember without questions or interruptions. So I brewed a simple cup of tea and tucked my remembrance inside the steam.

I sipped slowly, and the room felt like a soft pocket where only I could go. Respect for the past, privacy for the present.

WHEN TO PERFORM:

Early morning or after everyone is asleep

TIME TO ALLOT:

3 minutes

WHERE TO PERFORM:

Kitchen

INGREDIENTS/TOOLS:

- ◊ Mug
- ◊ Black tea bag
- ◊ Honey
- ◊ Ground cinnamon
- ◊ Water

🌙 Optional: A pinch of cocoa. Not required, but adds a deep, warm note for heart-comfort.

Directions

1. Place the tea bag in your mug and add hot water.
2. Stir in a little honey and a light dusting of cinnamon.
3. Cup the mug with both hands and whisper, "I remember in my own quiet."
4. Breathe the steam, sip three times, and keep your thought between you and the cup.
5. Rinse the mug when done, imagining any heavy feeling washing away.

Soft Goodbye Spell for Processing Loss

Some goodbyes are slow and shapeless. I kept waiting for the right words that never arrived. One evening, I used an apple slice and honey to say what my voice could not.

The sweetness did not erase the ache, but it gave the ache a gentle place to rest. I felt myself release one small knot.

WHEN TO PERFORM:

Sunset or anytime you feel the wave rise

TIME TO ALLOT:

3 minutes

WHERE TO PERFORM:

Kitchen sink or counter

INGREDIENTS/TOOLS:

- ◇ Tea light candle
- ◇ Small bowl
- ◇ Water
- ◇ Apple slice
- ◇ Honey

🌙 Optional: A chamomile tea bag nearby for calm.

Directions

1. Fill the bowl with water and float the apple slice on top.
2. Drip a little honey onto the apple and light the candle beside it.
3. Say, "I bless what was. I let go with love."
4. Close your eyes, place a hand on your chest, breathe in for four, out for six.
5. Snuff the candle. Take the apple outside to compost or lay under a plant, then pour out the water.

Lineage Light Spell for Family Tension

Family can feel like a tangle of wires. Sparks, but also light. I needed a small ritual to cool the sparks and invite better words.

This little candle shifted the tone. Not magic that fixes people, just magic that softens the room so kindness has a chance.

WHEN TO PERFORM:

Before a call or visit, or on a Friday evening

TIME TO ALLOT:

3 minutes

WHERE TO PERFORM:

Kitchen table

INGREDIENTS/TOOLS:

- ◊ Tea light or taper candle
- ◊ Olive oil
- ◊ Sugar
- ◊ Bay leaf
- ◊ Water in a cup

☽ Optional: A pinch of dried rosemary for peace in conversation.

Directions

1. Rub a drop of olive oil on the candle from base to wick for gentle flow.
2. Sprinkle a little sugar around the candle to sweeten the mood.
3. Place the bay leaf under the candle holder and set the cup of water nearby to absorb heat.
4. Light the candle and say, "May our words be clear and kind."
5. Snuff the flame when you are done. Discard the sugar into the trash and the bay leaf into the water, then pour it out.

Shadow Pocket Spell for Guilt Patterns

Guilt can loop like a song you cannot turn off. I needed a place to park it so my brain could breathe. So I made a tiny pocket for my shadows.

Once sealed, the pressure eased. I could think again, and choose better.

WHEN TO PERFORM:

Waning moon or any Sunday night

TIME TO ALLOT:

3 minutes

WHERE TO PERFORM:

Kitchen counter

INGREDIENTS/TOOLS:

- ◊ Small jar with lid
- ◊ Coffee grounds
- ◊ Pinch of salt
- ◊ Lemon peel
- ◊ Water

☽ Optional: A single clove to lock the seal.

Directions

1. Add a spoon of coffee grounds to the jar for clarity and wakefulness.
2. Drop in the lemon peel for fresh release, then a pinch of salt for cleansing.
3. Pour in a little water, close the lid, and shake once.
4. Hold the jar and say, "I release what I cannot change. I keep what teaches me."
5. Set the jar under the sink for one day, then pour it out and rinse the jar for reuse.

Fresh Start Doorway Spell for Life Transitions

When life was shifting, my front door felt heavy, like it remembered every goodbye. I mixed a quick lemon wash and light, and the whole entrance breathed out.

Every time I walked through, it felt like walking into a clean page.

WHEN TO PERFORM:

Morning of a new chapter, new job, move, or first day of the month

TIME TO ALLOT:

3 minutes

WHERE TO PERFORM:

Front door or main entry

INGREDIENTS/TOOLS:

- ◊ Bowl
- ◊ Warm water
- ◊ White vinegar
- ◊ Lemon slice
- ◊ Tea light candle

☽ Optional: A pinch of baking soda for extra refresh.

Directions

1. In the bowl, mix warm water with a splash of vinegar and squeeze the lemon slice.
2. Light the candle nearby for bright energy.
3. Dip a clean cloth or paper towel into the mix and wipe the door frame and knob.
4. Say, "I step forward clear and ready."
5. Snuff the candle. Pour the leftover mix down the drain.

North Star Naming Spell for Goal Setting

I kept vague wishes that never landed. The shift came when I named one clear star to steer by. Simple, specific, spoken out loud.

This tiny ritual gave my goal a shape I could follow.

WHEN TO PERFORM:

New moon or Sunday at sunrise

TIME TO ALLOT:

3 minutes

WHERE TO PERFORM:

Kitchen table by a window

INGREDIENTS/TOOLS:

- ◊ Bay leaf
- ◊ Ground cinnamon
- ◊ Sugar
- ◊ Tea light candle
- ◊ Cup of water

Optional: A few rice grains to anchor steady progress.

Directions

1. Place the bay leaf in your palm and sprinkle a pinch of sugar and cinnamon on it.
2. Hold it near your lips and clearly speak one goal, "My north star is _____."
3. Light the candle. Gently pass the bay leaf through the air above the flame to warm it without burning.
4. Crumble the bay leaf into the water and say, "I choose the next right step."
5. Snuff the candle. Pour the water outside or into the sink to send the message onward.

Veil-Night Spell for Intuitive Decisions

When choices felt muddy, I watched water and ice. The way the edges formed told me what my gut already knew.

It is amazing how quiet answers appear when you give them a simple stage.

WHEN TO PERFORM:

Night of a tough decision, ideally after sunset

TIME TO ALLOT:

3 minutes

WHERE TO PERFORM:

Kitchen with the lights dimmed

INGREDIENTS/TOOLS:

- ◇ Mug
- ◇ Cold water
- ◇ One ice cube
- ◇ Tea light candle
- ◇ Pinch of salt

☽ Optional: A dash of nutmeg for wise guidance.

Directions

1. Pour cold water into the mug and add the ice cube.
2. Light the candle and sprinkle a tiny pinch of salt into the mug.
3. Ask your question out loud, then watch the melt pattern for a slow count of thirty.
4. Say, "What is true shows itself to me."
5. Sip a small taste. Notice the first calm answer that rises.

Hearth Welcome Spell for Safe Gatherings

Guests were coming, and I wanted warmth without chaos. I made a tiny simmer and let the kitchen speak hospitality for me.

The house felt cozy, like a hug at the door.

WHEN TO PERFORM:

An hour before friends arrive or during holidays

TIME TO ALLOT:

3 minutes to start the simmer

WHERE TO PERFORM:

Stovetop

INGREDIENTS/TOOLS:

- ◊ Small pot
- ◊ Water
- ◊ Orange peel
- ◊ Cinnamon stick or ground cinnamon
- ◊ Vanilla extract

Optional: Whole clove for protective warmth.

Directions

1. Fill the pot with water and set on low heat.
2. Add orange peel, a bit of cinnamon, and a drop of vanilla.
3. Stir once and say, "Only kindness and safety enter here."
4. Let it gently steam while you host. Add water as needed.
5. Turn off the heat when done and discard the contents.

Lantern of Self-Trust Spell for Confidence

I kept looking outside for yes or no. One night I chose to be my own lantern with lemon and honey by a single flame.

Confidence did not roar. It glowed. And that was enough.

WHEN TO PERFORM:

Before an interview, exam, or tough talk

TIME TO ALLOT:

3 minutes

WHERE TO PERFORM:

Kitchen counter

INGREDIENTS/TOOLS:

- ◊ Tea light candle
- ◊ Mug
- ◊ Warm water
- ◊ Lemon slice
- ◊ Honey

☽ Optional: A pinch of ginger for boldness.

Directions

1. Add warm water, a squeeze of lemon, and a little honey to the mug.
2. Light the candle and hold the mug close to your chest.
3. Take three slow breaths and say, "I trust my voice. I trust my choices."
4. Sip three times, feeling the warmth spread.
5. Snuff the candle and step forward with your answer.

Chapter 2: Ember Love Glow & Confidence

On Samhain nights, hearth fires once marked the edge of the village. People walked between flames to shed old worries and step into the season with clearer hearts. Lovers exchanged tokens, and some practiced trial marriages that could be renewed or released the next year. Love was sacred, but so were boundaries. The fire did not just warm. It defined a circle of safety and self.

This chapter borrows that wisdom. Your heart is a hearth. Let your glow attract what nourishes you, and let your edges protect your peace. These quick kitchen spells help you sort the swipes, speak with ease, set early boundaries, and trust your inner radar. Love others well. Love yourself first.

Your words are magick

If this book has sparked your craft, eased your heart, or reminded you that you are not alone on the path, would you leave a quick review?

Even a single sentence holds power. It takes only a moment, yet it helps this work reach more seekers who are searching for guidance and glow.

As an indie witchy author, your feedback is both a blessing and a beacon. It lifts my spirit and lights the way for others who need these spells of support.

Thank you for walking this circle with me.

Swipe Sift Spell for Dating Burnout

I first made this when the swipe blur had me forgetting what I actually wanted. Profiles felt like static and my gut had gone quiet. I salted the noise, woke it with coffee, and watched a steady yes or no rise from underneath the scroll. Since then, this tiny mix cuts through the haze fast. My attention comes home, my instincts speak up, and I exit the app before the app empties me.

WHEN TO PERFORM

Sunday evening or any waning moon

TIME TO ALLOT

3 minutes

WHERE TO PERFORM

Kitchen

INGREDIENTS/TOOLS

◊ Small bowl

◊ 1 teaspoon coarse salt

◊ 1 teaspoon coffee grounds

◊ 1 bay leaf

◊ 1 white tea light candle

☽ Optional: Add a pinch of rosemary.

Directions

1. Place the candle beside the bowl and light it.

2. Add salt and coffee to the bowl. Stir clockwise and say: "Wake my wise yes. Guard my gentle no."

3. Hold the bay leaf over the bowl and whisper one clear intention, like "I call aligned matches."

4. Pass the bay leaf through the candle's smoke, then tuck it near your phone or case.

5. Snuff the candle. Dispose of the mix in the trash to release digital drain.

Silence Ease Spell for Communication Gaps

I first made this when a read receipt sat like a pebble in my shoe and my mind sprinted miles past the facts. I brewed softness and let the steam loosen my grip. The worry thinned and a kinder question appeared. Since then, this cup reminds me that pauses are not verdicts, they are space, so I answer with calm and only what is true.

WHEN TO PERFORM

Wednesday night or anytime before reaching out

TIME TO ALLOT

3 minutes

WHERE TO PERFORM

Kitchen

INGREDIENTS/TOOLS

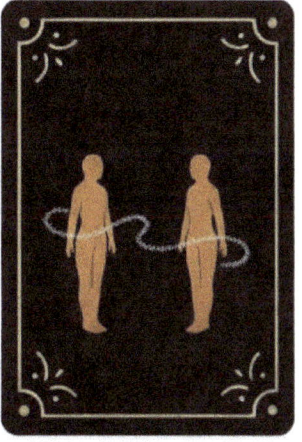

◇ Mug

◇ 1 cup hot water

◇ 1 chamomile tea bag

◇ 1 teaspoon honey

◇ 1 white candle

☽ Optional: Add a few lavender buds.

Directions

1. Light the candle. Steep the tea for about 2 minutes.
2. Stir in honey and whisper: "I speak with calm. I hear with care."
3. Hold the warm mug at your chest. Take three slow breaths.
4. Decide one kind question to ask or one truth to share.
5. Sip. Snuff the candle. Send the message if it still feels right.

Early Boundaries Spell for New Relationships

I first made this when a spark ran hot and my edges went fuzzy. I wanted the flutter without the freefall. I drew my line with leaf, salt, and a pinch of pepper, and felt my center click back in. Since then, I enter new chapters with sweetness and spine. Romance can be warm without melting my no.

WHEN TO PERFORM

First three dates or a new moon

TIME TO ALLOT

3 minutes

WHERE TO PERFORM

Kitchen

INGREDIENTS/TOOLS

- ◊ Small plate
- ◊ 1 bay leaf
- ◊ Pinch of table salt
- ◊ Pinch of black pepper
- ◊ 1 white candle

☽ Optional: Add a drop of olive oil.

Directions

1. Light the candle. Place the bay leaf on the plate.
2. Sprinkle a tiny ring of salt around the leaf for protection.
3. Add a light dusting of pepper at the north edge to signal a firm no.
4. Say: "What is kind to me is welcome. What is not cannot cross."
5. Pass the leaf through the smoke, then tuck it in your wallet or bag. Snuff the candle.

Release Shield Spell for Moving On

I first made this when the breakup was over but still humming under my skin. Every song and every street snagged me. Lemon, salt, and breath turned the residue to rinse water, and I watched it swirl away. Since then, when old cords tug, I clear, seal, and stand. What is gone stays gone, and my peace holds.

WHEN TO PERFORM

At sunset during a waning moon or any evening you feel ready

TIME TO ALLOT

3 minutes

WHERE TO PERFORM

Kitchen

INGREDIENTS/TOOLS

- ◇ Small bowl
- ◇ 1 cup water
- ◇ 1 lemon wedge
- ◇ 1 teaspoon salt
- ◇ 1 white candle

🌙 Optional: Add a few rose petals.

Directions

1. Light the candle. Squeeze the lemon into the water: salt, and stir counterclockwise.
2. Say: "I release the past. I seal my peace."
3. Dip your fingertips and touch your wrists and heart space.
4. Take three breaths, then pour the bowl down the sink.
5. Snuff the candle. Step outside if you can and feel the air on your skin.

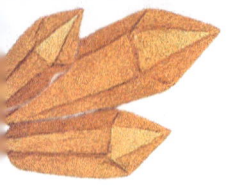

Bridge Spell for Cultural Differences

I first made this after a dinner where small misunderstandings piled into a quiet wall. Rice, bread, and salt made a path across the table. We walked it with stories and laughter, and the stiffness softened. Since then, I set this bridge before tough crossings. Honor opens doors that explanations alone cannot.

WHEN TO PERFORM

Before a shared meal or on Thursday

TIME TO ALLOT

3 minutes

WHERE TO PERFORM

Kitchen

INGREDIENTS/TOOLS

◇ **Small handful uncooked rice**

◇ **Slice of bread**

◇ **Pinch of salt**

◇ **1 cup water**

◇ **1 white candle**

☽ Optional: Add a drizzle of olive oil.

Directions

1. Light the candle. Place the bread on the counter.

2. Make a small line of rice from the bread toward the place you will sit, like a tiny bridge.

3. Sprinkle a pinch of salt on the bread and say: "Different roots. Shared table. Kind hearts."

4. Sip a little water and offer a sip to your guest later if appropriate.

5. Snuff the candle. Serve the bread with your meal.

Social Ease Spell for Meeting New People

I first made this with nerves rattling my ribs on the way to a room of strangers. Mint brightened my edges, orange lifted my mood, and sugar reminded me to be sweet to myself. Since then, three sips turn the pressure down. I arrive curious, not performative, and people meet me where I actually am.

WHEN TO PERFORM

One hour before going out or on Friday

TIME TO ALLOT

3 minutes

WHERE TO PERFORM

Kitchen

INGREDIENTS/TOOLS

- ◊ Mug
- ◊ 1 mint tea bag
- ◊ 1 cup hot water
- ◊ Orange peel or thin orange slice
- ◊ 1 teaspoon sugar

☽ Optional: Add a few fresh mint leaves.

Directions

1. Steep mint for about 2 minutes. Add sugar and swirl in the orange.
2. Say: "I am warm. I am welcome. I meet welcome."
3. Take three sips. With each sip, imagine your chest glowing soft and steady.
4. Save the orange peel in your pocket for a quick confidence sniff on arrival.

Glow Confidence Spell for Special Events

I first made this when a big night loomed and I feared I would burn too hot or flicker out. Honey and cinnamon warmed me from the inside. No spotlight chase, just a steady ember. Since then, this glaze settles me into enough. I shine without strain, and the room comes closer.

WHEN TO PERFORM

Before dates, interviews, or celebrations

TIME TO ALLOT

3 minutes

WHERE TO PERFORM

Kitchen

INGREDIENTS/TOOLS

- ◇ Small bowl
- ◇ 1 teaspoon honey
- ◇ 1 pinch ground cinnamon
- ◇ 1 teaspoon water
- ◇ 1 red candle

🌙 Optional: Add a drop of vanilla extract.

Directions

1. Light the candle. Mix honey, cinnamon, and water into a light glaze.
2. Say: "I glow with calm courage. My presence is enough."
3. Dab a tiny bit on wrists and over your heart.
4. Smile at your reflection in any shiny surface.
5. Snuff the candle. Head out while the warmth lingers.

Clear Voice Spell for Honest Conversations

I first made this before a talk I had postponed into dread. Peppermint cleared the doorway, lemon cut the fog, honey smoothed the path, and my truth stepped forward without armor. Since then, this brew is my pregame for candor. Direct, gentle, and impossible to tangle.

WHEN TO PERFORM

Wednesday morning or before an important call

TIME TO ALLOT

3 minutes

WHERE TO PERFORM

Kitchen

INGREDIENTS/TOOLS

- ◊ Mug
- ◊ 1 peppermint tea bag
- ◊ 1 cup hot water
- ◊ 1 lemon wedge
- ◊ 1 teaspoon honey

Optional: Add a pinch of grated ginger.

Directions

1. Steep peppermint briefly. Squeeze lemon and stir in honey.
2. Hover your hand over the mug and say: "Clear words. Kind tone. True heart."
3. Take three mindful sips.
4. Speak your main point out loud once to practice. Go make the call.

Reframe Spell for Handling Criticism

I first made this when feedback pricked every bruise and I wanted to shrink. Black tea grounded me, milk and sugar softened the sting, and cinnamon nudged me toward the lesson inside the sting. Since then, I sort gold from gravel fast. I keep the useful, compost the rest, and keep moving.

WHEN TO PERFORM

After receiving feedback or on Monday morning

TIME TO ALLOT

3 minutes

WHERE TO PERFORM

Kitchen

INGREDIENTS/TOOLS

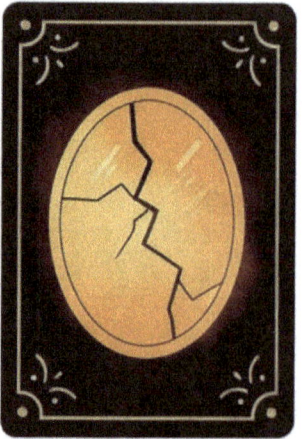

- ◊ Mug
- ◊ 1 black tea bag
- ◊ 1 cup hot water
- ◊ Splash of milk
- ◊ 1 teaspoon sugar or honey

 Optional: Add a pinch of ground cinnamon.

Directions

1. Steep tea to medium strength. Add milk and sugar.
2. Stir clockwise and say: "I keep the lesson. I release the sting."
3. Take three sips. After each, name one strength you showed.
4. Write one small improvement you will try today, then move on.

Safety Radar Spell for First Meetings

I first made this before coffee with a stranger, when intuition whispered but anxiety shouted. Vinegar, salt, and a bay leaf tuned the dial. The noise dropped and my body's yes or no came through crisp. Since then, I do this before any first meet. If a red flag flaps, I leave early and trust the quiet that warned me.

WHEN TO PERFORM

Before heading out to meet someone new

TIME TO ALLOT

3 minutes

WHERE TO PERFORM

Kitchen

INGREDIENTS/TOOLS

- ◊ 1 white candle
- ◊ 1 cup water
- ◊ 1 teaspoon white vinegar
- ◊ Pinch of salt
- ◊ 1 bay leaf

🌙 Optional: Add a clove of garlic to the bowl.

Directions

1. Light the candle. Mix water, vinegar, and salt in a cup.
2. Dip your fingertips and touch your wrists and the back of your neck.
3. Hold the bay leaf and say: "Body speak clear. I trust and act."
4. Tuck the leaf in your pocket. Snuff the candle.
5. If any red flags arise later, step away. Your first no is your best shield.

Money & Prosperity "Track the trickles and the river finds you."

On Samhain nights, villagers watched for the sleek shadow of a black cat crossing their path. Far from bad luck, the cat was a secret messenger. If it paused at your doorstep, the tale said a hidden fortune was near. People left bowls of cream and crumbs by the threshold, a tiny offering to invite soft-pawed blessings and keep scarcity outside the door.

Another Samhain custom tucked coins into loaves and porridge. Whoever found the hidden piece was said to catch the flow of the coming year's wealth. That is the heart of prosperity magic. You do not force the river. You notice the trickles, honor them, and build a channel. Each small choice becomes a current. Each spell below is a gentle paw-tap toward that current.

Budget Sweep Spell for Hidden Expenses

I first made this spell after my card statement gave me a jump scare. Tiny subscriptions and "just this once" charges piled up like dust bunnies. I felt silly for missing them, but shame does not pay bills. Focus does.

That night I lit a small candle, salted my space, and breathed slow. I pictured money as a kitchen floor. One steady sweep, then another. By the time the flame cooled, I had a short list of sneaky charges to cancel. It felt like cracking a window and letting in fresh air.

WHEN TO PERFORM:

Saturday or during the waning moon

TIME TO ALLOT:

12 minutes

WHERE TO PERFORM:

Kitchen counter or table

INGREDIENTS/TOOLS:

- ◊ White candle
- ◊ Salt
- ◊ Ground cinnamon
- ◊ Bay leaf
- ◊ Water

 Optional: Add dried basil.

Directions

1. Light the white candle. Sprinkle a thin ring of salt on the table to mark your focus zone.

2. Pinch cinnamon into the ring and say, "Reveal what nibbles at my coin."

3. Dip the tip of the bay leaf in water. With your fingernail, lightly etch three words on the leaf: "fees, subs, leaks."

4. Hold the leaf over the candle's warmth and whisper, "Little costs, show your names. I choose where money remains."

5. Place the leaf beside you. Breathe three slow breaths and picture a clean kitchen floor.

6. Real world action: open your recent statements and cancel

at least one charge today.

Refund Recall Spell for Overlooked Returns

I made this when I realized I never sent back a sweater that did not fit. The return window was close, and I felt annoyed at myself. Rather than spiral, I stirred a tiny cup of kitchen magic to pull attention to what I was owed.

The ritual felt like fishing with bright bait. Within an hour, I found two return credits I had missed. It was not a windfall, but it reminded me of something better. I do not have to chase money. I can call it home.

WHEN TO PERFORM:

Wednesday or Thursday during a waxing moon

TIME TO ALLOT:

10 minutes

WHERE TO PERFORM:

Kitchen

INGREDIENTS/TOOLS:

- ◊ Green candle
- ◊ Lemon
- ◊ White sugar
- ◊ Black coffee grounds
- ◊ Water

☽ Optional: Add a sprig of mint.

Directions

1. In a small cup: a spoon of water and a pinch of coffee grounds. Swirl clockwise.
2. Squeeze a few drops of lemon into the cup, then add a pinch of sugar.
3. Light the green candle and say, "Credits due, refunds owed, circle back along this road."
4. Take three slow breaths, then dab a fingertip in the sweet coffee and tap your wrist.
5. Sip a tiny taste, then pour the rest down the sink to release the call.

6.   Real world action: check your email and orders for return labels, and submit at least one return or credit request right now.

Boundary Spell for Shared Finances

I made this when sharing bills felt like tiptoeing around eggshells. The conversations were foggy. Lines were fuzzy. That fuzziness costs money and peace.

This boundary ritual gave me a calm center. After it, I could say, "This is mine, that is yours, and here is our shared middle," without heat. We set dates and amounts. No more surprise storms.

WHEN TO PERFORM:

Saturday evening or the day after a new moon

TIME TO ALLOT:

15 minutes

WHERE TO PERFORM:

Kitchen table

INGREDIENTS/TOOLS:

- ◊ White candle
- ◊ Salt
- ◊ Black pepper
- ◊ Olive oil
- ◊ Bay leaf

Optional: Add dried rosemary.

Directions

1. Anoint the candle with a drop of olive oil from base to tip. Light it.

2. Make a small circle of salt on the table. Sprinkle a light dusting of black pepper along the circle's edge.

3. With your fingernail, mark the bay leaf with three lines: "mine, yours, ours."

4. Hold the leaf over the flame's warmth and say, "Clear lines, kind words, steady plan."

5. Place the leaf at the circle's center and tap it three times.

6. Real world action: write down who pays which bill, the exact amount, and the due dates. Share it kindly and keep a copy where you both see it.

Raise Request Spell for Courageous Asking

I brewed this when my stomach jittered at the thought of asking for a raise. I had the receipts of my value, but my voice felt small.

The sweetness and spice steadied me. I walked into the talk with warm confidence, not a hard edge. My words were clear. My ask was direct. Courage is not loud. It is steady.

WHEN TO PERFORM:

Thursday morning or during a waxing crescent

TIME TO ALLOT:

12 minutes

WHERE TO PERFORM:

Kitchen

INGREDIENTS/TOOLS:

- ◊ Orange or white candle
- ◊ Ground cinnamon
- ◊ Honey
- ◊ Lemon
- ◊ Water

☽ Optional: Add fresh ginger.

Directions

1. In a cup: warm water, a squeeze of lemon, a drizzle of honey, and a pinch of cinnamon. Stir clockwise.

2. Light the candle and say, "My work has weight. My voice has worth."

3. Take three slow sips. Feel your throat relax and your back lengthen.

4. Rub a tiny bit of honey on your wrist and say, "I ask with grace. I receive with ease."

5. Snuff the candle.

6. Real world action: write one clear sentence of your ask and one sentence of proof. Send the meeting request today.

Reminder Spell for Late Payments

Late fees ate my snacks that month. Not dramatic, just annoying. I needed a gentle system with a little magic to make it stick.

This thyme ritual turned reminders into a rhythm. Late fees stopped. Relief arrived in the form of quiet.

WHEN TO PERFORM:

Monday morning or on a new moon

TIME TO ALLOT:

10 minutes

WHERE TO PERFORM:

Kitchen

INGREDIENTS/TOOLS:

- ◊ White candle
- ◊ Dried thyme
- ◊ White sugar
- ◊ Salt
- ◊ Water

🌙 Optional: Add a bay leaf.

Directions

1. Place a spoon of water in a cup. Add a pinch of dried thyme.
2. Sprinkle a pinch of sugar and a pinch of salt. Stir clockwise.
3. Light the candle and say, "Time, be kind. Bills, align."
4. Dip your fingertip in the thyme water and tap the table three times as you speak your main due date out loud.
5. Take a mindful sip.
6. Real world action: set at least two reminders for each bill date you named. One a week before, one two days before.

Clarity Spell for Big Purchases

My brain buzzed about a major purchase. I wanted it, but did I need it now? The swirl was loud.

This lemon clarity spell sliced through the fog. The answer felt clean. I either waited without FOMO or bought with peace.

WHEN TO PERFORM:

Sunday afternoon or during a waxing gibbous

TIME TO ALLOT:

12 minutes

WHERE TO PERFORM:

Kitchen with natural light

INGREDIENTS/TOOLS:

- ◊ White candle
- ◊ Lemon
- ◊ Bay leaf
- ◊ Uncooked rice
- ◊ Water

☽ Optional: Add dried sage.

Directions

1. Pour a small mound of rice on the table. Place the unlit candle behind it like a sunrise.

2. Add a spoon of water to a cup with a squeeze of lemon.

3. Light the candle and hold the bay leaf above the cup's steam. Say, "Cut through want. Show me need."

4. Look at the candle through the rice mound. If the flame looks steady, timing is right. If it flickers or feels off, wait.

5. Place the bay leaf under the rice for one hour to seal the decision.

6. Real world action: if you wait, set a date to review. If you buy, write the exact budget line it comes from.

Calm Spell for Financial Paperwork

Stacks of forms can turn my pulse jumpy. I used to avoid them, which only made the stack grow teeth.

I made a gentle cup that tasted like a soft blanket. I sat, sipped, and the stack stopped being a monster. Pages got done.

WHEN TO PERFORM:

Monday evening or any quiet night

TIME TO ALLOT:

15 minutes

WHERE TO PERFORM:

Kitchen table

INGREDIENTS/TOOLS:

◊ Chamomile tea bag

◊ Honey

◊ Milk

◊ White candle

◊ Vanilla extract

 Optional: Add a pinch of nutmeg.

Directions

1. Make a warm cup of chamomile with a splash of milk, a drizzle of honey, and a tiny drop of vanilla.

2. Light the candle and say, "Paper turns plain. My mind stays calm."

3. Hold the cup with both hands. Breathe in for four, out for six, three times.

4. Take three slow sips.

5. Snuff the candle and start on the first page for just five minutes.

6. Real world action: finish at least one form tonight, even if imperfect.

Patience Spell for Long-Term Goals

I wanted results fast, but savings grow like seeds, not fireworks. My impatience felt like picking at a sprout.

This simple ritual taught my hands to wait. Patience is not passive. It is steady care.

WHEN TO PERFORM:

First Sunday of the month or during a waxing moon

TIME TO ALLOT:

12 minutes

WHERE TO PERFORM:

Kitchen altar or counter

INGREDIENTS/TOOLS:

- ◊ Uncooked rice
- ◊ Ground cinnamon
- ◊ Honey
- ◊ Green candle
- ◊ Water

🌙 Optional: Add a bay leaf under the rice.

Directions

1. Make a small hill of rice. Drizzle a thin line of honey from base to tip.
2. Sprinkle cinnamon like morning light over a field.
3. Wet your finger with a drop of water and press the top of the hill.
4. Light the green candle behind the rice and say, "I grow with time. I keep my climb."
5. Sit for one minute picturing your goal as a full jar.
6. Real world action: move a small set amount into savings today. Do it every week, no matter how small.

Beacon Spell for Networking Opportunities

I used to dread "networking." Then I reframed it as sending out a warm light that said, "I am here. I can help."

This bright orange spell turned my energy from shy to inviting. People reached back. Doors opened a crack.

WHEN TO PERFORM:

Friday noon or at sunrise

TIME TO ALLOT:

10 minutes

WHERE TO PERFORM:

Kitchen with a sunny window

INGREDIENTS/TOOLS:

- ◊ Orange
- ◊ Ground cinnamon
- ◊ White sugar
- ◊ White candle
- ◊ Water

☽ Optional: Add a few fresh mint leaves.

Directions

1. Twist off a strip of orange peel and curl it into a little spiral.
2. Make a thin sugar circle on the table. Place the peel in the center. Dust with a tiny pinch of cinnamon.
3. Touch your finger to water and tap the peel three times.
4. Light the candle and say, "I shine. The right people find me."
5. Hold the peel to your nose and breathe in confidence.
6. Real world action: send one friendly message today to someone you respect, offering a simple hello or a helpful link.

Leak Finder Spell for Draining Habits

My money did not vanish. It trickled out in little habits. A snack here, a scroll there, a ride I did not need.

This kitchen bowl became a mirror. I saw which habits were itching to be replaced. Not shamed, just seen.

WHEN TO PERFORM:

Saturday during a waning moon

TIME TO ALLOT:

12 minutes

WHERE TO PERFORM:

Kitchen sink or counter

INGREDIENTS/TOOLS:

- ◇ White candle
- ◇ Vinegar
- ◇ Water
- ◇ Salt
- ◇ Black pepper

☽ Optional: Add dried sage beside the bowl.

Directions

1. In a bowl: water with a splash of vinegar.
2. Sprinkle a line of salt across the surface.
3. Add a pinch of black pepper and watch where it drifts through the salt.
4. Light the candle and say, "Leaks reveal. I choose to seal."
5. Notice the path the pepper takes. Name one habit for each path you see.
6. Real world action: create one replacement now. Prep a snack at home, set a rideshare limit, or make a weekly treat budget.

Black Cat Tip: Small wins compound. Every refund found, every boundary set, every patient deposit turns your kitchen table into a steady altar of wealth. Keep playing. Keep tracking the trickles. The river will find you.

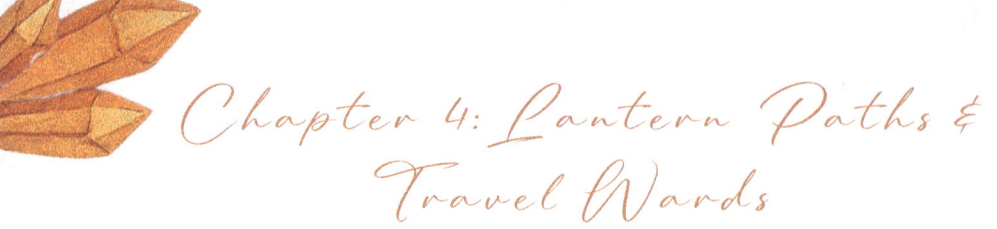

Chapter 4: Lantern Paths & Travel Wards

"Carry your own lantern, mind and map."

On Samhain nights long ago, travelers in the mist watched for flickers of will o' the wisps that danced across bogs and crossroads. Some said the lights were mischievous spirits trying to lure the unwary off the safe path. Others believed they were ancestor lanterns, guiding the living toward right choices when the road split and nerves trembled. In Ireland and Scotland, turnips were carved into grim little lanterns to scare off what wandered in the dark and to mark the way home.

Witches learned simple wards for the road. A pinch of salt at the doorway. Iron by the gate. A candle lit before setting out, then snuffed when returning, to close the path cleanly. These small rituals stitched the journey to the self, like a thread that keeps a button from falling off. In this chapter, you carry your own lantern. Mind and map in one hand. Quick spells to steady your voice, mark your scope, choose a path, pack what matters, and land softly wherever you go.

Steady Hands Spell for High-Stakes Tasks

I made this on the morning of a nerve rattling exam when my hands would not quit shaking. I sweetened water with a little honey and pinched in salt, whispering that my body knew what to do. The first sip felt like a hush. Since then, it is my pre performance drink. Simple, warm, and grounding. My hands remember the rhythm. My mind remembers I am safe.

WHEN TO PERFORM:

Morning of the task or a Saturday

TIME TO ALLOT:

7 minutes

WHERE TO PERFORM:

Kitchen counter or table

INGREDIENTS/TOOLS:

- ◇ Clear glass
- ◇ Water
- ◇ Honey
- ◇ Pinch of sea salt
- ◇ Small white tealight

🌙 Optional: Add a fresh ginger slice

Directions

1. Clear the surface and wash your hands slowly.
2. Pour water into the glass. Add honey and salt, stirring clockwise.
3. Light the tealight. Hold the glass with both hands and breathe deep.
4. Say, "Hands be steady. Heart be ready. I move with calm."
5. Take three slow sips, feeling warmth spread into fingers and chest.
6. Snuff the candle. Rinse the glass and go do the thing.

Fluency Flow Spell for Public Speaking

Before a speech I once nearly bailed on, I brewed peppermint tea with lemon and honey. I breathed in the steam and pictured my words sliding like a river over smooth stones. By the time I stepped up, my voice felt clear. The tea had already taught my mouth to flow.

WHEN TO PERFORM:

An hour before speaking or a Wednesday

TIME TO ALLOT:

10 minutes

WHERE TO PERFORM:

Kitchen

INGREDIENTS/TOOLS:

- ◊ Mug
- ◊ Hot water
- ◊ Peppermint tea bag
- ◊ Lemon slice
- ◊ Honey

🌙 Optional: Add a pinch of fresh mint leaves

Directions

1. Cleanse your space with a quick wipe and steady breath.
2. Pour hot water over the tea bag in the mug.
3. Add lemon and honey. Stir clockwise while setting your intention.
4. Hold the mug under your chin and say, "Voice flow free. Words serve me."
5. Sip slowly, imagining cool green light moving through your throat.
6. Finish the cup. Save the last sip to touch your lips before you begin speaking.

Rhythm Spell for Presentations

I used to rush through slides like I was being chased. One day I made a tiny shaker with rice in a jar, tapped a steady beat, and matched my breath to it. My pace dropped into a groove. Now, before any presentation, I set my rhythm on purpose. People lean in, and I finish with air to spare.

WHEN TO PERFORM:

The night before or a Thursday

TIME TO ALLOT:

8 minutes

WHERE TO PERFORM:

Kitchen table

INGREDIENTS/TOOLS:

- ◊ Small jar with lid
- ◊ Uncooked rice
- ◊ Cinnamon stick
- ◊ White tealight
- ◊ Water

 ☽ Optional: Add a clove to the jar

Directions

1. Put a spoonful of rice and the cinnamon stick in the jar. Close the lid.
2. Light the tealight. Place a small bowl of water nearby to ground the space.
3. Shake the jar gently to find a comfortable beat.
4. Speak one key sentence of your talk to that beat.
5. Say, "I keep time. Time keeps me." Repeat three times while tapping.
6. Snuff the candle. Keep the shaker near your notes for go time.

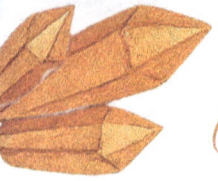

Compass Spell for Project Scope

I once agreed to everything and delivered nothing. Then I learned to draw a circle small enough to finish. A pinch of salt, a bay leaf, and pepper taught me the magic word no. Now, before projects, I set my compass so I ship what I promise.

WHEN TO PERFORM:

New moon or Monday morning

TIME TO ALLOT:

9 minutes

WHERE TO PERFORM:

Kitchen counter

INGREDIENTS/TOOLS:

◊ Small plate

◊ Sea salt

◊ Bay leaf

◊ Black pepper

◊ White tealight

🌙 Optional: Add a tiny drop of olive oil on the bay leaf

Directions

1. Sprinkle salt on the plate in a neat circle no bigger than your hand.

2. Place the bay leaf in the center. Light the tealight.

3. Pinch black pepper onto the outside of the circle to mark what is out of scope.

4. Say, "This circle is what I will do. All else waits outside."

5. Touch the bay leaf and name the top three deliverables out loud.

6. Snuff the candle. Keep the bay leaf with your plan as a living boundary.

Fit Spell for Career Choices

Big fork in the road. Two offers. My head spun. I made a simple sweet and salty test on a plate. Apple, sugar, salt. My body voted first. My mind followed. That day I picked the path that tasted like yes.

WHEN TO PERFORM:

Sunrise or Friday

TIME TO ALLOT:

6 minutes

WHERE TO PERFORM:

Kitchen

INGREDIENTS/TOOLS:

- ◇ Small plate
- ◇ Apple slice
- ◇ Sugar
- ◇ Sea salt
- ◇ White tealight

🌙 Optional: Add a sprinkle of cinnamon

Directions

1. Light the tealight. On the plate, pour sugar on the left and salt on the right.

2. Hold the apple slice over the center. Think of Choice A, then Choice B.

3. Say, "Body know true. Guide me through."

4. Drop the apple. Notice which side it leans toward first and how your mouth feels when you imagine each choice.

5. Taste a tiny bit of sugar, then salt, while imagining each path. Watch your body's yes or no.

6. Snuff the candle. Write your decision and take one small step today.

Focus Spell for Planning and Prep

On my most scattered days, rosemary and lemon cut through the fog. I built a clear glass ritual to plan the next three steps, not the next three years. It makes the day bite sized. Chew, swallow, win.

WHEN TO PERFORM:

Sunday evening or first thing Monday

TIME TO ALLOT:

10 minutes

WHERE TO PERFORM:

Kitchen table

INGREDIENTS/TOOLS:

◊ Clear glass

◊ Water

◊ Sprig of rosemary or pinch dried

◊ Lemon peel

◊ White tealight

☾ Optional: Add three ice cubes to seal focus

Directions

1. Fill the glass with water. Add rosemary and lemon peel.
2. Light the tealight. Hold the glass at eye level.
3. Say, "Mind like glass. Plans that last."
4. Sip once. Speak your top three tasks clearly.
5. Trace a small clockwise circle over the glass with your finger to seal.
6. Snuff the candle. Keep the glass nearby until the first task is done, then pour it out as a reset.

Check Loop Spell for Travel Essentials

I used to forget chargers and socks like it was my job. Beans fixed it. Thirteen beans, one small loop, one pass per item. Nothing slips the circle. Packing stopped being chaos. It became a clean click.

WHEN TO PERFORM:

The night before travel

TIME TO ALLOT:

8 minutes

WHERE TO PERFORM:

Kitchen counter

INGREDIENTS/TOOLS:

- ◊ Plate
- ◊ Small bowl
- ◊ 13 dry beans
- ◊ Pinch of sea salt
- ◊ White tealight

 Optional: Add a bay leaf under the bowl for protection

Directions

1. Light the tealight. Sprinkle salt in a thin ring on the plate.
2. Place the bowl in the center. Put all 13 beans in the salt ring.
3. Name 13 must pack items. For each one you place in your bag, move one bean from the ring into the bowl.
4. Say, "What I need moves with me." Repeat as you finish.
5. If any beans remain, those are the items to double check.
6. Snuff the candle. Pour the beans into a pocket for safe travels.

Calm Spell for Shared Spaces

New dorm. Noisy Airbnb. Tense office. I learned to make peace with vinegar water, vanilla, and a small light. The room softened like a held breath letting go. Now any place can become my place.

WHEN TO PERFORM:

Upon arrival or Saturday afternoon

TIME TO ALLOT:

9 minutes

WHERE TO PERFORM:

Kitchen and then the shared space

INGREDIENTS/TOOLS:

◊ Small bowl of water

◊ Splash of white vinegar

◊ Drop of vanilla extract or pinch cinnamon

◊ Clean cloth or paper towel

◊ White tealight

☽ Optional: Add a lavender sprig

Directions

1. Mix water, vinegar, and vanilla in the bowl.
2. Light the tealight in the center of the room.
3. Dampen the cloth and wipe door handles or a small surface you touch often.
4. Say, "This space holds ease. I enter in peace."
5. Stand still for three breaths, feeling the room exhale with you.
6. Snuff the candle. Let the scent linger.

Reset Spell for Energy Shifts

After a rough meeting, I used to carry the static all day. Now I slice an apple, dust cinnamon, and sweeten the moment. I eat the reset and step back into my life clean. It is a tiny ritual with a big turn.

WHEN TO PERFORM:

After hard conversations or sunset

TIME TO ALLOT:

5 minutes

WHERE TO PERFORM:

Kitchen

INGREDIENTS/TOOLS:

- ◊ Apple slice
- ◊ Cinnamon
- ◊ Honey
- ◊ Small plate
- ◊ White tealight

Optional: Add a few sunflower seeds for bright mood

Directions

1. Light the tealight. Place the apple slice on the plate.
2. Dust with cinnamon and drizzle a little honey.
3. Say, "Old charge go. Fresh start grow."
4. Take three slow bites, imagining static dissolving with each one.
5. Cup the candle's warmth to your heart, then your throat, then your head.
6. Snuff the candle. Wash the plate and carry the reset forward.

Sync Spell for Time Differences

Jet lag used to make me feel like a ghost in my own body. I built a tiny tonic to nudge my clock. It tastes like sunrise even at midnight. Now I land in new time zones with more ease.

WHEN TO PERFORM:

On arrival or the night before travel

TIME TO ALLOT:

7 minutes

WHERE TO PERFORM:

Kitchen or hotel kitchenette

INGREDIENTS/TOOLS:

- ◊ Black tea bag
- ◊ Hot water
- ◊ Pinch of sugar
- ◊ Pinch of sea salt
- ◊ Lemon slice

🌙 Optional: Add a few ice cubes if adjusting to earlier mornings

Directions

1. Brew the tea to medium strength.
2. Add sugar, salt, and lemon. Stir clockwise for waking up, counterclockwise for winding down.
3. Say, "Body align. I keep new time."
4. Sip slowly while looking at the local clock for one full minute.
5. Take three deep breaths, syncing inhale and exhale with a steady count of four.
6. Finish the cup. Get sunlight or dim light to match your goal.

Carry your lantern, traveler. Salt your thresholds. Choose your circles. And when the road bends, let your small rituals point you where your feet can follow.

Chapter 5: Hearth, Friends, Family

"Hold your center; weave the thread you can carry."

On Samhain nights, old hearths were the heart of the home. Families banked the fire, shared bread, and set a spirit place at the table to honor the ones who once sat there. The living and the dead met at the threshold, and the doorway became a sacred line between worlds. The message was simple and steady: keep your flame, guard your home, welcome what is kind.

In the myths, hospitality carried power. A humble bowl of salt could promise peace, and a candle in the window could guide a traveler to safety. The hearth taught balance. Share generously, yet keep the pot safely tended. In our busy lives, that lesson still works. These spells help you soothe schedules, draw kind people, set clean boundaries, and create a warm circle without losing yourself.

Harmony Spell for Scheduling Conflicts

I first made this spell on a week when my phone buzzed like a hornet nest. Triple-booked, guilt heavy, I grabbed a lemon from the fridge and a glass from the cabinet, because my brain needed a fresh start. I salted the water, stirred three times, and spoke one clear priority.

By the last swirl, the knot in my chest loosened. Calls got moved, one plan stayed, and the day felt breathable again. It did not add hours. It gave me focus.

WHEN TO PERFORM:

Sunday evening or on a new moon

TIME TO ALLOT:

3 minutes

WHERE TO PERFORM:

Kitchen counter

INGREDIENTS/TOOLS:

- ◊ Clear glass
- ◊ 1 cup water
- ◊ 1 lemon slice
- ◊ Pinch of salt
- ◊ Teaspoon

🌙 Optional: Add a bay leaf

Directions

1. Clean your counter and rinse the glass.
2. Pour the water: the salt, and drop in the lemon slice.
3. Stir clockwise three times and say, "I choose what matters most today."
4. Name out loud your top one to three commitments.
5. Hold the glass to your heart for one breath, then sip.
6. Schedule or release the rest with calm clarity.

Boundary Spell for Lending & Borrowing

I once kept saying yes to lending things, then felt resentful when they returned late or dented. I mixed salt and vinegar in a small bowl, set a candle behind it, and drew a circle that said, "I can be generous without being a doormat."

The next time someone asked, I said yes with a deadline and a smile. They brought it back on time. The circle held.

WHEN TO PERFORM:

Tuesday or during a waning moon

TIME TO ALLOT:

3 minutes

WHERE TO PERFORM:

Kitchen table

INGREDIENTS/TOOLS:

- ◊ Small bowl
- ◊ 2 tablespoons white vinegar
- ◊ Pinch of salt
- ◊ Pinch of black pepper
- ◊ White tea light candle
- ☽ Optional: Add a clove

Directions

1. Place the bowl on the table and pour in the vinegar.
2. Add salt and pepper, swirling counterclockwise once to set limits.
3. Set the tea light behind the bowl and light it safely.
4. Say, "I share with care. What I lend returns whole and on time."
5. Visualize clear terms and a kind tone.
6. Let the candle burn while you text or note your return date, then snuff.

Open Doors: Hello Spell for New Neighbors

When new neighbors moved in, I felt shy. I mixed a quick sweet lemon water, traced a tiny heart on the doorframe, and practiced my one-line hello.

Minutes later, I walked over with a smile that felt real. We chatted about trash day and local pizza. A small gesture, a warm start.

WHEN TO PERFORM:

Friday or during a waxing crescent

TIME TO ALLOT:

3 minutes

WHERE TO PERFORM:

By your front door

INGREDIENTS/TOOLS:

◊ Small bowl

◊ 1 teaspoon sugar

◊ 1 teaspoon lemon juice

◊ 2 tablespoons water

◊ 1 bay leaf

☽ Optional: Add a drop of vanilla

Directions

1. Mix water, sugar, and lemon in the bowl until dissolved.

2. Float the bay leaf and say, "My door welcomes good company."

3. Dip your fingertip and trace a small heart on the inside doorframe.

4. Rehearse a simple line, like, "Hi, I am next door. Welcome."

5. Pocket the bay leaf as a pocket charm.

6. Go say hello within the day.

Ask With Ease: Ease Spell for Asking Help

Asking for help used to feel like swallowing gravel. One night, I stirred honey into chamomile and spoke the request I had been avoiding.

By the last sip, the words softened. I asked the next day and heard, "Of course."

WHEN TO PERFORM:

Monday morning or first quarter moon

TIME TO ALLOT:

3 minutes

WHERE TO PERFORM:

Kitchen

INGREDIENTS/TOOLS:

- ◊ Mug
- ◊ 1 chamomile tea bag
- ◊ 1 cup hot water
- ◊ 1 teaspoon honey
- ◊ Pinch of cinnamon

 Optional: Add a sprig of fresh mint

Directions

1. Place the tea bag in the mug and pour hot water.
2. Stir in honey and a light dusting of cinnamon.
3. Hold the mug and say, "Help asked with grace is help received."
4. Sip slowly while you speak your exact request out loud.
5. Picture the person saying yes, or offering an honest alternative.
6. Send the message or schedule the ask while the mug is warm.

Grace Spell for Stepping Back from Groups

I felt stretched thin in a group chat that never slept. A brisk peppermint cup helped me release pressure without guilt.

I wrote a short, kind note, stepped back for a season, and my peace returned.

WHEN TO PERFORM:

Saturday or during a waning moon

TIME TO ALLOT:

3 minutes

WHERE TO PERFORM THIS SPELL:

Kitchen sink

INGREDIENTS/TOOLS:

- ◇ Mug
- ◇ 1 peppermint tea bag
- ◇ 1 cup hot water
- ◇ 1 lemon slice
- ◇ Pinch of salt
- ☽ Optional: Add a few rose petals

Directions

1. Steep the peppermint tea: the lemon, and a tiny pinch of salt.
2. Say, "I release what drains. I keep what nourishes."
3. Sip half while visualizing space returning to your week.
4. Carry the rest to the sink.
5. Pour it out slowly as you picture a graceful exit message.
6. Send or schedule the message with a kind tone.

Steady Nerves: Calm Spell for First Impressions

Before a big meeting, my hands shook. I made a quick sugar-water rinse and a crisp apple swipe that felt like a reset button.

I walked in steady, not perfect, yet present.

WHEN TO PERFORM:

Morning of the event or a waxing moon

TIME TO ALLOT:

3 minutes

WHERE TO PERFORM THIS SPELL:

Kitchen

INGREDIENTS/TOOLS:

- ◇ Small bowl
- ◇ 2 tablespoons water
- ◇ 1 teaspoon sugar
- ◇ 1 apple slice
- ◇ Paper towel

 Optional: Add a pinch of ground ginger

Directions

1. Dissolve sugar in the water in a small bowl.
2. Dip the apple slice and swipe lightly over your wrists and throat.
3. Say, "I arrive as myself, calm and clear."
4. Pat dry with the paper towel.
5. Stand with feet hip-width, breathe in for four, out for six.
6. Go make your introduction within the hour.

Bridge Spell for Difficult Conversations

I once dreaded a talk that could have gone rough. I mixed a drop of sugar into olive oil and anointed my throat, then held a bay leaf over water as a promise to stay cool.

The conversation was honest. It was also kinder than I expected.

WHEN TO PERFORM:

Wednesday or during a waxing moon

TIME TO ALLOT:

3 minutes

WHERE TO PERFORM THIS SPELL:

Kitchen table

INGREDIENTS/TOOLS:

- ◊ Small dish
- ◊ 1 teaspoon olive oil
- ◊ 1 pinch sugar
- ◊ 1 bay leaf
- ◊ 1 cup water
- ☽ Optional: Add a dash of vanilla

Directions

1. In the dish, blend the olive oil with a pinch of sugar.
2. Touch a fingertip to the blend and anoint your throat and heart.
3. Hold the bay leaf above the cup of water and say, "May my words be honest and heard."
4. Place the bay leaf beside the dish.
5. Take one sip of water to cool your voice.
6. Have the conversation soon after.

Circle Spell for Building New Friendships

After moving, I felt like an extra chair at someone else's table. I made a tiny cinnamon sugar circle with a spark of light and an orange peel smile.

Within days, I joined a game night. It felt easy, like doors clicked open.

WHEN TO PERFORM:

Thursday afternoon or during a waxing moon

TIME TO ALLOT:

3 minutes

WHERE TO PERFORM THIS SPELL:

Kitchen counter

INGREDIENTS/TOOLS:

- ◊ Small plate
- ◊ 1 teaspoon sugar
- ◊ 1 pinch ground cinnamon
- ◊ 1 strip orange peel
- ◊ White tea light candle
- ☽ Optional: Add a few sunflower seeds

Directions

1. Sprinkle sugar in a small circle on the plate.
2. Dust cinnamon over the circle and place the orange peel in the center.
3. Set the tea light beside the plate and light it safely.
4. Say, "I meet good people and they meet me."
5. Name one place or event you will show up to this week.
6. Snuff the candle and keep the peel in your pocket when you go.

Cooldown Spell for Heated Moments

During an argument, my thoughts ran hot. I grabbed a glass, ice, mint, and lemon. The cold sip chilled my temper enough to hear what was actually being said.

No winner or loser, just a pause that saved the day.

WHEN TO PERFORM:

Any time tempers flare

TIME TO ALLOT:

3 minutes

WHERE TO PERFORM THIS SPELL:

Kitchen

INGREDIENTS/TOOLS:

- ◊ Glass
- ◊ Ice cubes
- ◊ 1 cup water
- ◊ 1 mint tea bag
- ◊ 1 lemon slice

☽ Optional: Add a pinch of sugar

Directions

1. Add ice to the glass and pour in water.
2. Dip the mint tea bag a few times to cool the water with scent.
3. Squeeze the lemon slice, drop it in.
4. Say, "Cool head, warm heart, clear words."
5. Take three slow sips, breathing deeply between each.
6. Return to the talk only when your shoulders drop.

Ground Rules Spell for Shared Visits

Before hosting, I used to dread the chaos. One quick threshold wash with vinegar, soda, and lemon turned my doorway into a polite filter.

Guests arrived, had fun, and respected the space. So did I.

WHEN TO PERFORM:

The morning guests arrive or during a waning gibbous

TIME TO ALLOT:

3 minutes

WHERE TO PERFORM THIS SPELL:

By the front door

INGREDIENTS/TOOLS:

- ◊ Bowl
- ◊ 1 cup warm water
- ◊ 1 tablespoon white vinegar
- ◊ 1 teaspoon baking soda
- ◊ 1 teaspoon lemon juice
- Optional: Add a pinch of dried rosemary

Directions

1. In the bowl, combine warm water, vinegar, baking soda, and lemon.
2. Stir gently while saying, "Welcome kindly. Respect lives here."
3. Dip a clean cloth or paper towel you already have and wipe the threshold.
4. Stand at the door and visualize the visit going smoothly.
5. Smile as you open the door, grounded and clear.
6. Pour leftover wash outside your doorstep.

Hearth note:

Spells do not replace honest talks, clear texts, and real plans. They help you center, choose, and follow through. Keep your flame, and let good company gather around it.

Chapter 6: Cauldron of Health and Healing

Tend the vessel that carries your spark. Long before kitchens gleamed with steel, the cauldron was the heart of the home. In Samhain lore, the cauldron is a symbol of rebirth and repair, a simple pot that turns scraps into nourishment and tired spirits into steady ones. Legends of Cerridwen's cauldron speak of a brew that imparts wisdom and transformation. The message is plain and strong. Heal the vessel, and what it carries can shine again.

At Samhain, the veil thins and the body whispers truths we usually miss. The old ways say to listen for those whispers while stirring something warm, grounding, and kind. Season changes can jolt our rhythms. The antidote is simple care repeated with intention. A mug, a spoon, a steady breath. That is everyday witchcraft.

Soothe Spell for Social Exhaustion

I made this when my smile felt glued on and my ears hummed from too many conversations. The quiet of my kitchen felt like a blanket. Steam rose, and with it went the leftover noise.

Sip by sip, my shoulders dropped. I remembered I do not have to be on all the time. I can choose softness and recharge.

WHEN TO PERFORM

Sunday night or any evening after a busy day

TIME TO ALLOT

3 minutes

WHERE TO PERFORM

Kitchen

INGREDIENTS/TOOLS

- ◊ Mug
- ◊ Hot water
- ◊ Chamomile tea bag
- ◊ Honey
- ◊ Lemon slice

🌙 Optional: Add rose petals.

Directions

1. Hold the mug and take a slow breath. Say what you need to release.
2. Add the tea bag, pour hot water, and swirl in honey.
3. Float the lemon slice and watch the surface calm.
4. Whisper, "Quiet returns to me. I choose rest."
5. Sip slowly. With each swallow, imagine noise dissolving into steam.

Lift Spell for Seasonal Blues

The first cool morning hit and my mood slid gray. I needed a small sun I could make myself. So I built one on the stove.

Citrus and spice filled the air. It was like opening a window in my chest. Enough light to keep going.

WHEN TO PERFORM

Morning on cloudy days or during the waxing moon

TIME TO ALLOT

3 minutes

WHERE TO PERFORM

Kitchen

INGREDIENTS/TOOLS

- ◊ Small pot
- ◊ Water
- ◊ Orange peel
- ◊ Ground cinnamon
- ◊ Vanilla extract

☽ Optional: Add a strip of fresh ginger.

Directions

1. Add water to the pot with orange peel, a pinch of cinnamon, and a drop of vanilla.
2. Warm until fragrant. Stand over the gentle steam.
3. Inhale for four counts, exhale for six.
4. Say, "Light within me rises warm and steady."
5. Let the room hold that scent while you set one small goal for the day.

Boundary Spell for News Overload

I was refreshing headlines like a habit I could not shake. My attention felt frayed and jumpy. I needed a fence, not another article.

This little salt-and-vinegar rite reset my edges. After it, the phone went face down, and my mind felt mine again.

WHEN TO PERFORM

Any morning, or when the news starts to spiral

TIME TO ALLOT

3 minutes

WHERE TO PERFORM

Kitchen counter or entryway

INGREDIENTS/TOOLS

- ◊ Small bowl
- ◊ Table salt
- ◊ White vinegar
- ◊ Water
- ◊ Bay leaf

 Optional: Add a sprig of rosemary.

Directions

1. In the bowl, mix a spoon of salt with a splash each of vinegar and water.
2. Trace a small circle on the counter with your finger dipped in the mixture.
3. Press the bay leaf to your heart, then place it in the center of the circle.
4. Say, "I choose what enters. I choose what stays."
5. Wipe the circle clean, face the door, and put your phone in another room for one hour.

Anchor Spell for Daily Routines

My days felt slippery, like trying to hold water. I craved a simple anchor I would actually use. Coffee became the hook.

The glass on my counter turned into a daily lighthouse. Small, steady, and easy to keep.

WHEN TO PERFORM

Dawn or the night before a busy day

TIME TO ALLOT

3 minutes

WHERE TO PERFORM

Kitchen

INGREDIENTS/TOOLS

- ◊ Clear glass
- ◊ Water
- ◊ Coffee beans
- ◊ Rolled oats
- ◊ Honey

🌙 Optional: Add a vanilla bean tip.

Directions

1. Fill the glass halfway with water.
2. Drop in a few coffee beans for focus and a pinch of oats for steady energy.
3. Stir in a touch of honey clockwise.
4. Say, "I show up. I follow through."
5. Place the glass where you will see it after you wake. Each morning, touch it and name your top three tasks. Refresh daily.

Release Spell for Stress Tension

My jaw ached and my shoulders lived by my ears. I needed heat and breath and a short, kind pause.

This ginger steam softened everything. I felt my face unclench like a fist remembering how to open.

WHEN TO PERFORM

Evening or after work

TIME TO ALLOT

3 minutes

WHERE TO PERFORM

Kitchen

INGREDIENTS/TOOLS

- ◊ Small pot
- ◊ Water
- ◊ Fresh ginger slices
- ◊ Lemon slice
- ◊ Sea salt

☽ Optional: Add eucalyptus leaves.

Directions

1. Simmer water with a few ginger slices and a pinch of sea salt.
2. Remove from heat. Add the lemon slice.
3. Lean over the pot at a safe distance and breathe the steam in slowly.
4. On each exhale, whisper, "I lct go."
5. Roll your shoulders and unclench your jaw as you breathe.

Ease Spell for Waiting Anxiety

Waiting for a message made minutes feel like hours. My thoughts ran laps. A warm mint cup called them back.

The first sip slowed time enough to remember I can breathe here. Waiting can be gentle.

WHEN TO PERFORM

Anytime you are waiting, or during a new moon

TIME TO ALLOT

3 minutes

WHERE TO PERFORM

Kitchen or desk

INGREDIENTS/TOOLS

- ◊ Mug
- ◊ Hot water
- ◊ Peppermint tea bag
- ◊ Sugar
- ◊ Spoon

🌙 Optional: Add a sprig of fresh mint.

Directions

1. Brew peppermint tea lightly.
2. Stir in a little sugar counterclockwise to release restless energy.
3. Hold the mug with both hands and say, "I am safe while I wait."
4. Take three mindful sips, then place the mug down and stretch your fingers and neck.
5. Check your phone only after the tea is finished.

Listening Spell for Body Awareness

I kept ignoring the small signals. Thirst. Tight calves. A sigh that meant more than air. I decided to eat with my ears.

An apple on a plate turned into a tiny lesson. My body speaks. I can listen.

WHEN TO PERFORM

Before meals or bedtime

TIME TO ALLOT

3 minutes

WHERE TO PERFORM

Kitchen table

INGREDIENTS/TOOLS

- ◇ Apple slice
- ◇ Pinch of salt
- ◇ Ground cinnamon
- ◇ Small plate
- ◇ Napkin

☽ Optional: Add a drizzle of plain yogurt.

Directions

1. Place the apple slice on the plate. Sprinkle a tiny bit of salt and cinnamon.

2. Sit, feet on the floor. Take a slow breath and ask, "What do you need right now"

3. Take one small bite. Notice texture, temperature, flavor.

4. Put the bite down. Place your hand on your belly and listen for any signal.

5. Finish the slice with gratitude, or save it if your body says enough.

Break Spell for Screen Fatigue

My eyes burned like tiny suns. I kept scrolling anyway. Then I remembered I own water and tea bags, not just apps.

A cool compress reset the day. After three minutes, the world had softer edges.

WHEN TO PERFORM

Midday or whenever your eyes feel strained

TIME TO ALLOT

3 minutes

WHERE TO PERFORM

Desk or kitchen sink

INGREDIENTS/TOOLS

- ◊ Small bowl
- ◊ Cold water
- ◊ Two black tea bags
- ◊ Clean cloth
- ◊ Lemon slice

🌙 Optional: Add a few cucumber rounds.

Directions

1. Soak the tea bags in cold water for one minute, then gently squeeze.
2. Lay back or lean back, place cooled tea bags over closed eyes.
3. Rest the clean cloth across your forehead, breathe slow.
4. Say, "Clarity returns. Screens wait for me."
5. After two minutes, remove and rub a bit of lemon on your palms for a bright reset. Wash hands.

Gratitude Spell for Body Kindness

I was hard on my body for being tired. That never helped. I tried kindness instead, and everything softened.

A quick sugar and oil rub turned into a thank you note. My hands understood first.

WHEN TO PERFORM

Evening after a shower or before bed

TIME TO ALLOT

3 minutes

WHERE TO PERFORM

Bathroom or kitchen sink

INGREDIENTS/TOOLS

◊ Olive oil

◊ Granulated sugar

◊ Small bowl

◊ Warm water

◊ Towel

Optional: Add a pinch of ground turmeric.

Directions

1. Mix one spoon of sugar with a little olive oil in the bowl.
2. Rub gently into your hands or forearms in circles.
3. As you rub, say three thank yous to your body for what it did today.
4. Rinse with warm water and pat dry.
5. Cup your hands over your heart and breathe.

Return Spell for Gentle Recovery

After illness or burnout, I wanted to rush back. My body asked for bread and honey, not a sprint. So I listened.

This simple bite felt like walking barefoot on soft grass. Slow, sweet, and enough.

WHEN TO PERFORM

Morning during recovery days or waning moon

TIME TO ALLOT

3 minutes

WHERE TO PERFORM

Kitchen

INGREDIENTS/TOOLS

- ◊ Slice of bread
- ◊ Honey
- ◊ Ground cinnamon
- ◊ Small plate
- ◊ Cup of warm water

🌙 Optional: Add a few blueberries.

Directions

1. Place the bread on the plate. Drizzle honey and dust lightly with cinnamon.
2. Hold the plate at your heart and say, "I return with kindness."
3. Take small bites, sip warm water between them.
4. After eating, place your palm on your belly and promise one gentle task only.
5. Rest for one minute before moving on.

Remember, your body is your first cauldron. Tend it daily, and your spark burns clear.

Chapter 7: Witch's Protection Shield & Boundaries

On Samhain, folks pressed salt into door frames and set a crust of bread on the threshold. It was a soft but serious message to the night. Loved ones, come in. Tricksters, pass by. Boundaries were blessings that kept the hearth warm and the path clear. Turnips were carved into lanterns to scare off trouble. Hearth fires were relit for fresh luck, and travelers carried bay leaves for safe passage. The lesson still stands: ward first, wander later. When you set your boundaries, the world meets you with better behavior.

Guard Spell for Deliveries & Packages

Packages used to disappear from my stoop like socks in a dryer. I felt watched, exposed, and a little silly for caring so much about a box of vitamins and cat toys. One night, I mixed a quick door ward that smelled like a cozy café. The next week felt different. The entry had a hush to it, like a store after closing time. My boxes waited untouched, like they had their own polite "do not disturb" sign.

WHEN TO PERFORM

Morning, dusk, or during a waxing moon

TIME TO ALLOT

3 minutes

WHERE TO PERFORM

Front door or mailbox area

INGREDIENTS/TOOLS

- ◊ Salt
- ◊ Coffee grounds
- ◊ Ground cinnamon
- ◊ Black pepper
- ◊ White tea light candle

🌙 Optionalfor the Fancy Witch To take this spell to the next level: star anise.

DIRECTIONS

1. Light the tea light. Never leave it unattended.
2. In your palm, blend a pinch each of coffee, cinnamon, pepper, and salt.
3. Hold the blend over the flame for one breath and say, "Only what is mine arrives in time."
4. Pinch a tiny amount across the outer threshold. Invisible is fine.
5. Snuff the candle and picture your doorway glowing with a quiet, amber shield.

Privacy Spell for Shared Mailboxes

Living with a shared mailbox taught me how nosy some humans can be. I hated that prickle at my spine when someone lingered by the slots a little too long. I made a tiny privacy seal for my key and handle. After that, the box felt like a closed book. My mail started arriving like it belonged to me, not the hallway.

WHEN TO PERFORM

Any weekday before picking up mail

TIME TO ALLOT

3 minutes

WHERE TO PERFORM

Kitchen, then at the mailbox

INGREDIENTS/TOOLS

- ◊ Water
- ◊ White vinegar
- ◊ Salt
- ◊ Sugar
- ◊ Bay leaf

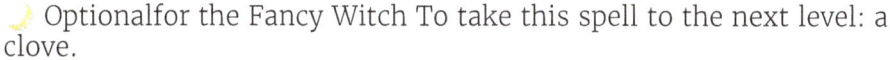 Optionalfor the Fancy Witch To take this spell to the next level: a clove.

DIRECTIONS

1. In a small cup, mix a splash of vinegar with water.
2. Dip a fingertip into the mix and trace a small circle on your mailbox key.
3. Tap a tiny blend of salt and sugar onto the key, then press the bay leaf to it with your thumb for one breath.
4. At the mailbox, wipe the handle with the remaining vinegar water and say, "Eyes turn away, my words stay."
5. Pocket the bay leaf with your key.

Silence Spell for Spam & Unwanted Calls

There was a week where my phone rang like a haunted doorbell. "Potential spam" popped up so much I started answering with a sigh. I brewed a hush for my ringtone energy. The quiet that followed felt like stepping into a library. My attention came back to me.

WHEN TO PERFORM

Evening or during a waning moon

TIME TO ALLOT

3 minutes

WHERE TO PERFORM

Kitchen counter near your phone

INGREDIENTS/TOOLS

◇ Water

◇ Lemon

◇ Salt

◇ Honey

◇ White tea light candle

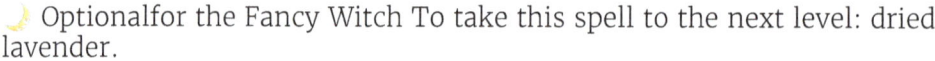 Optional for the Fancy Witch To take this spell to the next level: dried lavender.

DIRECTIONS

1. Light the candle safely.

2. Squeeze a few drops of lemon into a cup of water. Add a pinch of salt and a dab of honey. Stir clockwise.

3. Hold your phone above the cup and whisper, "Noise be still, only care can call."

4. Dab your fingertip in the mix and touch the top edge of your phone.

5. Snuff the candle and set the cup in the sink to drain.

Block Spell for Unwanted Contacts

Someone kept slipping back into my life like a pop-up ad. I needed a clean, swift block that felt final. I stirred this quick sink banish. It rinsed the sticky feeling right out of my day, like washing off a stamp you never asked for.

WHEN TO PERFORM

Anytime you feel intruded on

TIME TO ALLOT

3 minutes

WHERE TO PERFORM

Kitchen sink

INGREDIENTS/TOOLS

- ◊ Water
- ◊ White vinegar
- ◊ Salt
- ◊ Black pepper
- ◊ Coffee grounds

🌙 Optionalfor the Fancy Witch To take this spell to the next level: lemon peel.

DIRECTIONS

1. In the sink, pour a splash of vinegar. Add a pinch of salt, a pinch of pepper, and a pinch of coffee grounds.
2. Run a trickle of water to swirl the mix.
3. Say, "Your path ends here. I walk free and clear."
4. Let the water carry the blend away.
5. Dry your hands and move on. The block stands.

Cloak Spell for Leaving Safely

There are nights when the street feels like a stage and I would rather be backstage, unseen. This quick anointing turns you into quiet mist. People look past you, and the path opens like an automatic door.

WHEN TO PERFORM

Before leaving home, especially after sunset

TIME TO ALLOT

3 minutes

WHERE TO PERFORM

Entryway or kitchen

INGREDIENTS/TOOLS

- ◊ Olive oil
- ◊ Dried rosemary
- ◊ Black pepper
- ◊ Water
- ◊ White tea light candle

Optionalfor the Fancy Witch To take this spell to the next level: a bay leaf.

DIRECTIONS

1. Light the candle.
2. Place a drop of olive oil on your palm. Tap in a tiny pinch of rosemary and pepper.
3. Add one drop of water with your fingertip, rub palms, then dab wrists and the tops of your shoes.
4. Say, "I walk like fog, I pass unseen."
5. Snuff the candle and go.

Buffer Spell for Crowded Spaces

Crowds can feel like static against skin. Once, a train car had me breathing like a cornered cat. I made this quick drink and felt a bubble click into place. People still existed, but not on me.

WHEN TO PERFORM

Right before entering a crowd

TIME TO ALLOT

3 minutes

WHERE TO PERFORM

Kitchen or café table

INGREDIENTS/TOOLS

- ◊ Water
- ◊ Lemon
- ◊ Dried basil
- ◊ Salt
- ◊ Honey

 Optionalfor the Fancy Witch To take this spell to the next level: a mint leaf.

DIRECTIONS

1. In a cup, squeeze a little lemon. Add a pinch of basil, a whisper of salt, and a dab of honey.
2. Stir clockwise and breathe over the rim.
3. Say, "Circle of space, travel with me."
4. Sip three times.
5. Picture a clear, arm's-length bubble around you as you move.

Boundary Spell for Shared Kitchens

Shared kitchens can get political. My shelf became a negotiation I never agreed to. This ritual set a kind, firm line. No arguments needed. The space started behaving.

WHEN TO PERFORM

After tidying your area

TIME TO ALLOT

3 minutes

WHERE TO PERFORM

Kitchen counter and shelf

INGREDIENTS/TOOLS

◊ White vinegar

◊ Salt

◊ Sugar

◊ Ground cinnamon

◊ Bay leaf

Optionalfor the Fancy Witch To take this spell to the next level: vanilla extract.

DIRECTIONS

1. Dampen a cloth with vinegar and wipe your shelf or counter.

2. Mix a tiny pinch of salt with sugar and cinnamon, then dust a subtle line at the back edge of your space.

3. Press a bay leaf at the far corner and say, "This spot is mine, cared for and kind."

4. Breathe out and let the room reset.

Safeguard Spell for Pets & Doors

My anxious pup used to hover by the door like a tiny guard with no armor. I made a simple threshold blessing. The house felt calmer, and my pet stopped flinching at hallway noises.

WHEN TO PERFORM

Morning or before you leave

TIME TO ALLOT

3 minutes

WHERE TO PERFORM

Front or back door

INGREDIENTS/TOOLS

- ◊ Water
- ◊ Salt
- ◊ Dried rosemary
- ◊ Olive oil
- ◊ Bread crust

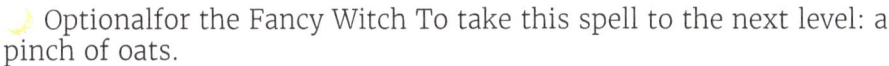 Optionalfor the Fancy Witch To take this spell to the next level: a pinch of oats.

DIRECTIONS

1. Mix a pinch of salt into a little water. With two fingers, trace a low line along the inside threshold.

2. Smudge a fingertip of olive oil with a bit of rosemary onto the doorknob, saying, "Only good crosses here."

3. Tuck a small bread crust just inside the doorframe as a guardian offering.

4. Give your pet a calm pat and breathe out.

Settle Spell for Nighttime Calm

Some nights my thoughts rattle like spoons in a drawer. Sleep feels far away and edgy. This warm sip dims the noise. The room feels heavy in the best way, like a blanket fresh from the dryer.

WHEN TO PERFORM

After sunset

TIME TO ALLOT

3 minutes

WHERE TO PERFORM

Kitchen, then bedside

INGREDIENTS/TOOLS

- ◊ Water
- ◊ Chamomile tea bag
- ◊ Honey
- ◊ Ground cinnamon
- ◊ White tea light candle

🌙 Optionalfor the Fancy Witch To take this spell to the next level: a slice of apple.

DIRECTIONS

1. Light the candle.
2. Steep the tea bag in hot water for a short minute. Stir in honey and a dust of cinnamon.
3. Hold the cup and say, "Body uncoil, mind grow still."
4. Sip slowly, then snuff the candle and rest.

Shield Spell for After-Hours Safety

Late nights can sharpen shadows. I used to clutch my keys like a talisman and still feel shaky. This key-shield rinse steadies your steps. It is a pocket-sized guardian that travels with you.

WHEN TO PERFORM

Before heading out after dark

TIME TO ALLOT

3 minutes

WHERE TO PERFORM

Kitchen sink or entryway

INGREDIENTS/TOOLS

- ◊ Water
- ◊ Salt
- ◊ Garlic clove
- ◊ Black pepper
- ◊ White tea light candle

 Optionalfor the Fancy Witch To take this spell to the next level: orange zest.

DIRECTIONS

1. Light the candle.
2. Crush a small bit of garlic between fingers and rinse them under water into a cup:ing a pinch of salt and pepper.
3. Hold your keys above the cup and say, "I am guided, guarded, and homebound."
4. Touch a drop of the water to the key head you hold when walking.
5. Pour the rest down the drain, snuff the candle, and carry your keys with calm shoulders.

Reminder: These spells are spiritual supports that complement practical safety. Lock doors, use delivery notes, block numbers, and trust your instincts. Your boundaries are sacred and effective.

Chapter 8: Autumn Hearth
Calm & Forgiveness

When the year leans into Samhain, old stories say the hearth becomes a living threshold. In Ireland and Scotland, families raked the last bonfire coals into a small ember and carried it home to restart their kitchen fire. That ember was more than heat. It was protection, blessing, and a promise that warmth survives the thin, windy nights. The hearth was where lost loved ones were welcomed, a seat pulled out at the table, a crust of bread set aside, steam rising like a quiet hello.

Another Samhain custom was the "dumb supper," a silent meal served for the ancestors. People moved gently, listened closely, and let memory soften sharp places. The lesson is simple. When the world feels noisy, you can choose to be the warm light you can carry. Calm is the ember. Forgiveness is the seat you pull out for yourself.

"Be the warm light you can carry."

Quiet Spell for Self-Doubt

I brewed this one after a rough day when every thought sounded like static. I lit a small candle on the counter, watched the flame steady itself, and felt my shoulders drop.

By the last sip, the criticism in my head shrank to a whisper. I could hear my real voice again, small but steady, like a pilot light catching.

WHEN TO PERFORM:

Sunday sunrise, or any new moon evening

TIME TO ALLOT:

7 minutes

WHERE TO PERFORM:

Kitchen counter or table

INGREDIENTS/TOOLS:

- ◇ Mug
- ◇ Hot water
- ◇ Chamomile tea bag
- ◇ Honey
- ◇ White tealight candle

☽ Optional: a pinch of dried lavender.

Directions

1. Tidy a small spot. Light the tealight.
2. Pour hot water over the chamomile.
3. Add a little honey, stir clockwise, and say, "Quiet the storm, grow the glow in me."
4. Hold the warm mug at your chest for three breaths.
5. Sip slowly. When finished, pinch out the candle and thank your calm.

Permission Spell for Fear of Success

I used to sabotage good news. Right before a win, I would trip myself with what ifs. One night I drew a circle in sugar and told myself I had full permission to grow.

It felt silly and perfect. I slept like a cat in sun and woke ready to claim my yes.

WHEN TO PERFORM:

Thursday night for expansion, or during a waxing moon

TIME TO ALLOT:

6 minutes

WHERE TO PERFORM:

Kitchen table

INGREDIENTS/TOOLS:

◊ Small bowl

◊ Granulated sugar

◊ Pinch of salt

◊ Vanilla extract

◊ White candle

☽ Optional: a pinch of ground turmeric for golden courage.

Directions

1. Pour sugar into the bowl. With your fingertip, trace a circle.

2. Touch a few grains of salt into the center and say, "I can hold success and stay true."

3. Add a drop of vanilla and breathe in sweetness.

4. Light the candle and look at the flame through the sugar circle.

5. Blow the candle out and keep a pinch of the sugar in your pocket for the day.

Peace Spell for Second-Guessing Decisions

After choosing a path, I used to pace and pick it apart. Lemon water became my reset. Simple, clear, and bright.

Sipping it, I realized peace is not perfect certainty. It is choosing once, then resting.

WHEN TO PERFORM:

Wednesday afternoon, or right after you make a decision

TIME TO ALLOT:

5 minutes

WHERE TO PERFORM:

Kitchen sink or table

INGREDIENTS/TOOLS:

- ◊ Glass
- ◊ Cold water
- ◊ Lemon slice
- ◊ Bay leaf
- ◊ Ice cube

Optional: a strip of lemon peel twist.

Directions

1. Fill the glass with cold water and add the ice.
2. Squeeze the lemon slice, then drop it in.
3. Float the bay leaf and say, "I chose, I rest, my mind is blessed."
4. Sip to the bottom, then remove the bay leaf and compost it.

Ease Spell for Pre-Result Anxiety

Waiting for test scores and emails used to knot my stomach. Warm milk with nutmeg turned the volume down.

It felt like a soft blanket for my nerves. I still do this before I check big news.

WHEN TO PERFORM:

Monday evening, or any time your chest tightens while waiting

TIME TO ALLOT:

10 minutes

WHERE TO PERFORM:

Stove or microwave station

INGREDIENTS/TOOLS:

- ◊ Small pot
- ◊ Milk or plant milk
- ◊ Honey
- ◊ Ground nutmeg
- ◊ White tealight candle

🌙 Optional: a tiny piece of vanilla bean or a drop of vanilla.

Directions

1. Warm the milk gently. Do not boil.
2. Stir in honey and a pinch of nutmeg.
3. Light the candle and hover your hands over the cup.
4. Say, "Ease in my body, calm in my mind."
5. Sip slowly. Let your shoulders drop with each breath. Blow out the candle when you feel settled.

Gate Spell for Information Overload

My brain used to feel like all the tabs were open at once. I made this little jar to be my filter.

It sits by my laptop, a reminder that not every fact gets a front-row seat.

WHEN TO PERFORM:

Any morning, or during a waning moon to reduce noise

TIME TO ALLOT:

8 minutes

WHERE TO PERFORM:

Kitchen counter

INGREDIENTS/TOOLS:

- ◊ Clean jar with lid
- ◊ Dry rice
- ◊ Salt
- ◊ Bay leaf
- ◊ Ground black pepper

Optional: a sprig of dried rosemary for clear recall.

Directions

1. Pour a handful of rice into the jar. This is all the incoming info.
2. Add a pinch of salt for boundaries.
3. Sprinkle a little black pepper to block distractions.
4. Slip in one bay leaf and say, "Only what matters passes my gate."
5. Cap the jar, shake gently, and set it beside your devices as a daily filter.

Apology Spell for Honest Repair

Before hard conversations, my mouth went dry and my pride got loud. This simple sweetening ritual helped me show up softer.

It did not erase the mistake. It made me brave enough to own it.

WHEN TO PERFORM:

Friday afternoon, or any day before you apologize

TIME TO ALLOT:

9 minutes

WHERE TO PERFORM:

Kitchen table

INGREDIENTS/TOOLS:

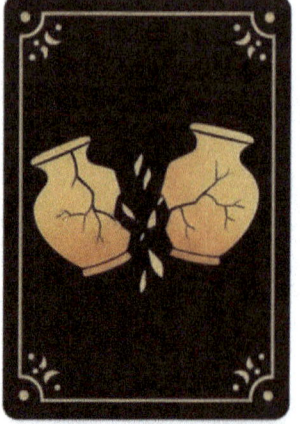

- ◊ Slice of bread
- ◊ Honey
- ◊ Cup of warm water
- ◊ Pinch of cinnamon
- ◊ White candle

☽ Optional: a few rose petals for compassion.

Directions

1. Drizzle a little honey on the bread.
2. Sprinkle cinnamon and say, "Sweet words, strong heart, truth with care."
3. Take a small bite to anchor the intention.
4. Sip warm water to cool defensiveness.
5. Light the candle for accountability, then blow it out and go make the apology.

Landing Spell for Life Transitions

When everything was changing at once, I felt floaty and thin. A bowl of salt, rice, and rosemary helped me land back in my body.

I finished the ritual feeling heavy in a good way, like roots finding soil.

WHEN TO PERFORM:

Saturday evening, or on the first night in a new place

TIME TO ALLOT:

7 minutes

WHERE TO PERFORM:

Kitchen counter or entry table

INGREDIENTS/TOOLS:

- ◊ Small bowl
- ◊ Warm water
- ◊ Pinch of salt
- ◊ Dry rice
- ◊ Dried rosemary

Optional: an orange peel for fresh beginnings.

Directions

1. Fill the bowl with warm water.
2. Add salt, rice, and a pinch of rosemary. Stir clockwise, then counterclockwise.
3. Hold your hands over the bowl and say, "I arrive. I belong. I am held."
4. Dip your fingertips in, touch your temples and the soles of your feet.
5. Pour the water outside or into a plant as a grounding offering.

Melt Spell for Guilt in Grief

Grief can carry sticky guilt. A simple cup of cocoa reminded me to meet my pain with warmth.

As the chocolate melted, some of the harshness did too.

WHEN TO PERFORM:

Sunday night, or any tender anniversary

TIME TO ALLOT:

10 minutes

WHERE TO PERFORM:

Kitchen

INGREDIENTS/TOOLS:

- ◊ Mug
- ◊ Hot water or warm milk
- ◊ Unsweetened cocoa powder
- ◊ Sugar
- ◊ Pinch of salt

Optional: a sprinkle of cinnamon for heart comfort.

Directions

1. Stir cocoa, sugar, and a pinch of salt into the hot water or warm milk.
2. Hold the mug and say, "I honor love. I release blame."
3. Sip slowly. If tears come, let them.
4. When finished, rinse the mug with gratitude.

Softening Spell for Missed Opportunities

I once watched an opportunity pass and felt my chest harden. This apple ritual softened the edges.

It reminded me that sweetness still exists, and more chances will ripen.

WHEN TO PERFORM:

Any evening during the waning moon

TIME TO ALLOT:

6 minutes

WHERE TO PERFORM:

Kitchen table

INGREDIENTS/TOOLS:

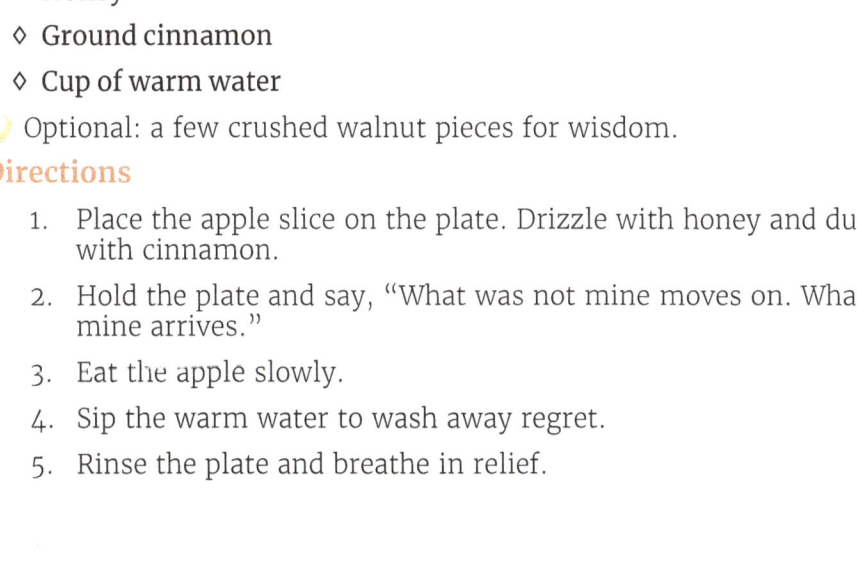

- ◇ Small plate
- ◇ Apple slice
- ◇ Honey
- ◇ Ground cinnamon
- ◇ Cup of warm water

🌙 Optional: a few crushed walnut pieces for wisdom.

Directions

1. Place the apple slice on the plate. Drizzle with honey and dust with cinnamon.
2. Hold the plate and say, "What was not mine moves on. What is mine arrives."
3. Eat the apple slowly.
4. Sip the warm water to wash away regret.
5. Rinse the plate and breathe in relief.

Grace Spell for Changing Your Mind

Changing my mind used to feel like failure. This tea taught me it can be grace.

I stirred out the first choice, stirred in the better one, and felt my spine relax.

WHEN TO PERFORM:

Any morning, or at the first tug to pivot

TIME TO ALLOT:

7 minutes

WHERE TO PERFORM:

Kitchen counter

INGREDIENTS/TOOLS:

- ◊ Mug
- ◊ Hot water
- ◊ Black tea bag
- ◊ Spoon
- ◊ Sugar

☽ Optional: a lemon twist for clarity.

Directions

1. Steep the tea to your liking.
2. Stir counterclockwise three times and say, "I release the path that no longer fits."
3. Stir clockwise three times and say, "I welcome the choice that serves me now."
4. Add sugar to sweeten the shift, then sip and move forward with ease.

Seasons Turn, Magick Remains

This book is not only for beginnings. It is meant to be your companion all year. When spring arrives and you feel the pull of growth, you can return here. When summer's energy burns bright and you want to shine with it, these pages will meet you. When autumn teaches balance and release, these spells will remind you how to let go with grace. When winter calls for stillness and reflection, you can come back to these simple rituals for comfort and clarity.

You do not have to read it once and set it aside. This is a spellbook to live with, to return to whenever you need grounding, protection, confidence, or love. Each time you open it, you may notice something new speaking to you, because magick works that way. It grows as you grow.

I am so grateful you allowed me to walk beside you in these first steps. Your path is your own, but it is an honor to share tools that make the journey a little lighter and a little brighter. May these spells remind you of your power, your worth, and your place in the circle of magick.

The truth is simple. You can return here anytime. The magick will be waiting for you.

Your words are magick

If this book has sparked your craft, eased your heart, or reminded you that you are not alone on the path, would you leave a quick review?

Even a single sentence holds power. It takes only a moment, yet it helps this work reach more seekers who are searching for guidance and glow.

As an indie witchy author, your feedback is both a blessing and a beacon. It lifts my spirit and lights the way for others who need these spells of support.

Thank you for walking this circle with me.

www.ingramcontent.com/pod-product-compliance
Lightning Source LLC
Chambersburg PA
CBHW071525120626

46550CB00006B/2365